VINTAGE
LIVING
TEXTS

Margaret Atwood

THE ESSENTIAL GUIDE
TO CONTEMPORARY
LITERATURE

The Handmaid's Tale
Bluebeard's Egg
The Blind Assassin

VINTAGE

Published by Vintage 2002

2 4 6 8 10 9 7 5 3 1

Copyright © Jonathan Noakes and Margaret Reynolds 2002

The right of Jonathan Noakes and Margaret Reynolds to be identified
as the authors of this work has been asserted by them in accordance with
the Copyright, Designs and Patents Act, 1988.

First published in Great Britain in 2002 by Vintage
Random House, 20 Vauxhall Bridge Road,
London SW1V 2SA

Random House Australia (Pty) Limited
20 Alfred Street, Milsons Point, Sydney,
New South Wales 2061, Australia

Random House New Zealand Limited
18 Poland Road, Glenfield,
Auckland 10, New Zealand

Random House (Pty) Limited
Endulini, 5A Jubilee Road, Parktown 2193, South Africa

The Random House Group Limited Reg. No. 954009
www.randomhouse.co.uk

A CIP catalogue record for this book is available from the British Library

ISBN 0 0994 3704 X

Papers used by Random House are natural, recyclable products made
from wood grown in sustainable forests; the manufacturing processes
conform to the environmental regulations of the country of origin.

Typeset by Palimpsest Book Production Limited, Polmont, Stirlingshire

Printed and bound in Great Britain by
Bookmarque Ltd, Croydon, Surrey

32252

CONTENTS

The Blind Assassin

VINTAGE LIVING TEXTS: REFERENCE

Acknowledgements

We owe grateful thanks to all at Random House. Most of all our debt is to Caroline Michel and her team at Vintage – especially Marcella Edwards – who have given us generous and unfailing support. Thanks also to Philippa Brewster and Georgina Capel, Michael Meredith, Angela Leighton, Harriet Marland, Louisa Joyner, Zara Warshal, to all our colleagues, and to our partners and families. We would also like to thank the teachers and students at schools and colleges around the country who have taken part in our trialling process, and who have responded so readily and warmly to our requests for advice. And finally, our thanks to Margaret Atwood for her work without whom . . . without which . . .

VINTAGE LIVING TEXTS

Preface

About this series

Vintage Living Texts: The Essential Guide to Contemporary Literature is a new concept in reading guides. Our aim is to provide readers of all kinds with an intelligent and accessible introduction to key works of contemporary literature. Each guide suggests techniques for reading important contemporary novels, and offers a variety of back-up materials that will give you ways into the text – without ever telling you what to think.

Content

All the books reproduce an extensive interview with the author, conducted exclusively for this series. This is not to say that we believe that the author's word is law. Of course it isn't. Once his or her book has gone out into the world he or she becomes simply yet another – if singularly competent – reader. This series recognises that an author's contribution may be valuable, and intriguing, but it puts the reader in control.

Every title in the series is author-focused and covers at

least three of their novels, along with relevant biographical, bibliographical, contextual and comparative material.

How to use this series

In the reading guides that make up the core of each book you will see that you are asked to do two things. One comes from the text; that is, we suggest what you should focus on, whether it's a theme, the language or the narrative method. The other concentrates on your own response. We want you to think about how you are reading and what skills you are bringing to bear in doing that reading. So this part is very much about you, the reader.

The point is that there are many ways of responding to a text. You could concentrate on the methods you might use to compare this text with others. In that case, look for the sections headed 'Compare'. Or you might want to do something more individual, and analyse how you are reacting to a text and what it means to you, in which case, pick out the approaches labelled 'Imagine' or 'Ask Yourself'.

Of course, it may well be that you are reading these texts for an examination. In that case you will have to go for the more traditional methods of literary criticism and look for the responses that tell you to 'Discuss' or 'Analyse'. Whichever level you (or your students) are at, you will find that there is something here for everyone. However, we're not suggesting that you stick solely to the approaches we offer, or that you tackle all of the exercises laid out here. Choose whatever most interests you, or whatever best suits your purposes.

Who are these books for?

Students will find that these guides are like a good teacher. They introduce the life and work of the author, set each novel in its context, explain key ideas and literary critical terms as they arise, suggest comparative exercises in a number of media, and ask focused questions to encourage a well-informed, analytical approach to reading the novels in a way that is rigorous, but still entertaining.

Teachers will find in this series a rich source of ideas for teaching contemporary novels and their contexts, particularly at AS, A and undergraduate levels. The exercises on each text have been tailored to meet the various assessment objectives laid down in the subject criteria for GCE AS and GCE A Level English Literature, and are explained in such a way that they can easily be selected and fitted into a lesson plan. Given the diversity of ways in which the awarding bodies have devised their specifications to meet these assessment objectives, a wide range of exercises is offered. We've had fun devising the plans, and we hope they'll be fun for you when you come to teach and learn with them.

And if you are neither a teacher nor a student of contemporary literature, but someone reading for your own pleasure? Well, if you've ever wanted someone to introduce you to a novelist's work in a way that will let you trust your own judgement and read more confidently, then this guide is also for you.

Whoever you are, we hope that you will enjoy using these books and that they will send you back to the novels to find new pleasures.

All page references to *The Handmaid's Tale* and *Bluebeard's Egg* in this text refer to the Vintage edition. Page references to *The Blind Assassin* refer to the Bloomsbury edition.

Margaret Atwood

Introduction

Margaret Atwood goes to some strange places. She keeps company with people who do strange things. She goes to places that even she knows nothing about. And she goes there with people she does not even know.

Atwood is a phenomenon. She is one of the most important writers of her generation. For more than twenty years she has published a body of work – novels, poetry and essays – that is consistently challenging, innovative, original, intelligent and uncompromising. She has won just about every prize going; she has been lauded and fêted with accolades. Her work has been translated into many languages and is read all over the world. It is created by a fiery intellect, but it also has tremendous popular appeal.

When we interviewed Atwood for this series, we asked her to tell us about the strangest episodes she could recall in which people – fans – had taken her books and used her themes or her arguments for their own purposes.

Atwood understood at once. 'Oh yes, yes,' she said:

There are some wonderful things like that. Actually there are several with cult followings of that kind.

One is *The Edible Woman* in which people make Edible Woman cakes, get their pictures taken around the cake, and then get pictures taken of themselves eating it, and then send me the pictures. In fact, I was in France for my birthday the year that they put *The Handmaid's Tale* on with More's *Utopia*, so I did a few little things, speeches on it. And the French are sentimental about birthdays, and I was at the Sorbonne and these French professors had made me an Edible Woman cake.

So there's that. People have dressed up as characters in *The Handmaid's Tale* quite a bit. They've dressed up in the costume. Usually in connection with book bannings, and things like that. And they will even, in a more frivolous way, dress up for costume parties.

Last Halloween, four people – not all of them women – arrived at my house dressed as the four characters from *The Robber Bride*. And I suppose it's really quite a compliment, because it means that the people in the book have taken on a life of their own in the popular imagination.

I'll tell you an unlikely thing to do with *The Handmaid's Tale*. When it first came out, someone went to the sea wall along Santa Monica, California Venice Beach. And they wrote, in big letters, 'The Handmaid's Tale is Here'. I know people who live there, they saw it.

I did a talk show in San Francisco when it first came out there – that would be 1985. And the presenter decided to be devil's advocate and said, 'Well, surely all of this is very silly? I mean, none of it will happen.' And the switchboard lit up. It just lit up like a Christmas tree with people phoning in saying, 'It's already happening.'

In some ways these sound like disconnected stories, but in fact they all tell us the same thing. For Atwood's readers, her fiction often seems to be about their own lives, or rather, it provides a way of thinking critically about the world and their place in the world.

There is a reason for this. On the one hand, Atwood's writings are grounded in acute observations of the physical world: the flowers, the clothes, the smells, the recipes, the landscapes, the weather – everything is vividly realised in the cocoon that is spun around the consciousness of her characters, even if (as in *The Handmaid's Tale*) we are intentionally disorientated with regard to the bigger picture. On the other hand, not one of Atwood's fictions comes to us just by itself. There is always another story behind the story, or inside the story, or reflected in the story. Pick any Atwood fiction, and you will see that one of her specialities is the remaking and revising of myths and archetypes. Sometimes it's fairy tales that she's rewriting, sometimes it's ancient Greek myth, or Romantic fiction, or Utopian fiction, or Gothic fiction. All of these have come under her scrutiny. So when a reader takes up one of her books, there is a background frame that means they know at once that this is a book about the stories that have made the world what it is. And therefore they also know that this is a book which will give them space to think about the world and what it is.

This is not to say that readers always need to know all the references and allusions that Atwood may be invoking. But sometimes when you find one, it can apply to different fictions too. For instance, the title story in Atwood's collection of short stories is 'Bluebeard's Egg' and it is a rewriting of the Bluebeard myth. But so is her novel *The Robber Bride* (1993), and the poem of the same name in her collection *Interlunar* (1984), and her novel *Lady Oracle* (1976). It's also possible to make a case for *The Handmaid's Tale* as a rewriting of the Bluebeard story, with the many wives, locked away, forbidden to know too much, used and discarded. It's possible also to make the same case for *The Blind Assassin*. In the fantasy world the mute girl has to submit, and in the 1930s world Richard Griffen keeps the keys to power and knowledge while his two 'wives', Iris and Laura, are denied choice in the matter of their own destiny. Atwood is interested in this particular fairy story because it says so much about men and women, and about curiosity and control. That's why she keeps reworking it. But it's also why readers recognise that her fiction can tell them true stories about power relations in the real world.

But if Atwood is a critic of Western culture and society, she is also a poet. She cares passionately about words and language and she knows how to use structure, shape and narrative pattern. In *The Handmaid's Tale*, one particular tragedy of Offred's situation is that she is forbidden to read, she is denied language. And yet Atwood makes that very denial the subject and focus of the novel, as Offred risks her life for the contraband word in her meetings with the Commander or, and even more importantly, in her insisting on telling herself or her imagined audience the story of her own existence: 'If it's a story, even in my head, I must be telling it to someone. You don't tell a story only to yourself. There's always someone else. Even when there is no one.'

Language is what shapes existence and experience, and the poet in Atwood knows that well. In *The Blind Assassin*, Alex and Iris explain their relationship to each other through the story of the planet Zycron, and Iris explains her own life to herself through the collage of her collected papers in the steamer trunk. In *Bluebeard's Egg*, the colloquial, haphazard tones of oral history explain characters and families and nations to themselves and to their listeners.

It may be that this interest in identity through expression is one to which Atwood is drawn because of her heritage as a Canadian writer. Of course, Atwood is first and foremost simply a writer – and a first-rate one – who needs no further qualification. But Atwood is a writer who is very conscious of the differences in national identities and how they can shape our reactions. She tells, for instance, how there were different reactions to *The Handmaid's Tale* in England, Canada and the United States: 'In England they said, "Jolly good tale." They had already done their religious theocracy, they had that under Oliver Cromwell. They weren't about to do it again right now. In Canada, in their anxious question-asking way, they said, "Could it happen here?" And in the United States, they said, "How long have we got?"'

There are certain ways in which Atwood's fictions and poetry exploit and explore her own national heritage and identity. The landscapes of *Cat's Eye* and *The Blind Assassin* are accurate representations of the ravines and bridges of Toronto that also translate into the richly evocative dream landscapes of the novels. The pioneering history of Canada lies behind many of Atwood's fictions, such as *Surfacing* or even *Bodily Harm*, and it's there in her poetry too, in *The Journals of Susanna Moodie* or in poems like 'Marrying the Hangman'. In a way it's also there in *The Handmaid's Tale* where there's a kind of historical rightness – as well as a hint of comic irony – in the fact that it is Canada that represents the place of safety, the place to which the persecuted escape from a corrupted United States.

If Canada gives Atwood a landscape, and a particular national history, and an interest in identity that is the legacy of any country whose heritage is one of emigration and displacement, it may be too that Canada gives Atwood a special way with language. It is, remember, a bilingual nation, so that nothing is ever definitive, there is always another way of putting things that is very typical of Atwood's interest in words. There is also such a thing as a certain dry, cool and understated Canadian wit, even if Atwood makes that entirely her own. On one occasion, when a large audience had gathered to hear Atwood read, the distinguished person chairing the proceedings began by introducing Atwood in fulsome terms, listing all her prizes and honours. Then she turned to Atwood and said, 'Have I left anything out?' Atwood replied, 'I can knit.'

It's a good story, a good joke. It also reveals one of the special ways in which Atwood's fiction (and poetry) works. Atwood knows her audience, and she excludes no one. The joke included the hundreds of people in that hall, just as her writings include everyone, are for everyone. If the poet in Atwood knows that words bring things into existence, she also knows the reader's contribution to that process. The shaping narrative patterns of repetition and revision, of metaphor and imagery, of assonance and word play, appear just as frequently in Atwood's fiction as they do in her poetry, and it's very much up to the reader to spot these connections and make intelligible shapes out of them. But Atwood knows that readers are all different, bringing different expertises and backgrounds to their readings, and that very consciousness means that she leaves no one out. Nor would she want to, because Atwood acknowledges that she needs her readers. As she says:

> When you read a book, it matters how old you are and when you read it and whether you're male or female, or from Canada or India. There is no such thing as a truly universal literature, partly because there are no truly universal readers. It is my contention that the process of reading is part of the process of writing, the necessary completion without which writing can hardly be said to exist.

Interview with Margaret Atwood

Hay on Wye: 26 May 2001

MR: It's almost impossible now to imagine a time when *The Handmaid's Tale* didn't exist. It's on numerous syllabuses, it's become a cultural reference point, something that people refer to and talk about. Can you remember now where the originating idea came from?

MA: I was talking to some friends and it was at the time of the rise of the religious right in the United States, when people were first realising that there was such a thing. Among the planks in that platform was 'women back to the home'. And I was saying that there are two things that have to be considered here: number one, with the type of people who say those things, if they get a chance to do it, they will; and number two, there's always the practical side of it. With all of these women running around outside of their homes, how are you going to stuff them all back in? How are you going to make them go back? Well, in effect, you do what Afghanistan has now done, in a very drastic way – you make it impossible for them to be anywhere else. And in Western society you would begin with the cancellation of their credit-card facilities. You know that moment when you put your card in, and it doesn't work. Well, think of that happening permanently, and on a gender-wide scale. So you would just reverse the various steps in the direction of more freedom for women that have taken place over the past hundred years or so. You would reverse each and every one of them, and then the women would be back in their homes, because they would have no other place to go.

That was one germ of the idea. There were two other beginnings of it. One was that I went from Canada to Harvard as a graduate student, and at that institution we had to write five comprehensive exams at the end of the first year, and they were for Departments of English literature, and one of American literature, and that was my gap. I had to fill that gap, so in my first year I studied intensively things that I would have to know for that examination, which included seventeenth- and eighteenth-century American literature. Now you may well say, 'What literature?' Well, I was studying the Puritans in the seventeenth century; I was studying their sermons, the odd poem – Anne Bradstreet, for instance; and I was studying the historical context of the sermons, and their personal journals. I was studying the civilisation, and it was clear to me that the United States did not begin as the bastion of liberty, freedom, equality and all of those eighteenth-century ideas. It began as seventeenth-century theocracy. It was totalitarian and hierarchical in nature. Those kinds of societies are always very interesting to look at. Some people mistakenly think that the society in *The Handmaid's Tale* is one in which all men have power, and all women don't. That is not true, because it is a true totalitarianism: therefore a true hierarchy. Those at the top have power, those at the bottom don't. And those at the bottom include men, and those at the top include women. The women at the top have different kinds of power from the power of the men at the top, but they have power nonetheless, and some of the power they have is power over other women, as is always the case in those kinds of societies. Like Serena Joy, like the

Aunts, the Aunt Lydias and so forth. That was the second germ of the idea. The third thing was that I had done a lot of reading in the area of utopias, dystopias and imagined societies, so I'd always been interested in that as a form. And it was a challenge.

MR: I remember you saying, when *The Handmaid's Tale* was published, that everything in the book either had happened in the world or was happening now. Do you feel any more cheerful about what's going on in the world now?

MA: Well, some of the things have since happened, as well as previously happening. These patterns have a horrible way of repeating themselves. For instance, we had not yet had the Baby M case at the time of *The Handmaid's Tale*. People thought that was the first surrogate motherhood, but of course it was no such thing. One of the first surrogate motherhoods is in the Bible, I quote it on the first page. It's the Rachel and Leah baby contest, in which the babies of each woman's handmaid got to count on their side of the score. So the twelve tribes of Israel were not produced from Rachel and Leah. They were produced from Rachel and Leah and their two handmaids. Anyway, we had not yet had Afghanistan [and the rule of the religious Taliban]; we had had Romania, where women were forced to have children, and we had had the events in Iran, where women were frequently put in those kinds of power positions over other women. So, I think more of the same has happened in very visible ways.

MR: You mention when you began writing *The Handmaid's Tale*, that you were reading about utopias and dystopias, and you quote a little bit from Jonathan Swift's *A Modest Proposal* as an epigraph. Sometimes *The Handmaid's Tale* is set against *Gulliver's Travels*. Could you comment on that?

MA: *Gulliver's Travels* is one of the great ancestors of these kinds of books as a genre. The thing to be noted about it is that Swift wrote it as a certain kind of social satire, but he did it so well, and in such pedestrian detail, that some people thought it was true. Similarly for *A Modest Proposal*, which is a piece of very acerbic satire. However, he did get some people who said, 'Actually that sounds like quite a good idea . . . let's cook and eat babies, it would help out with the population problem . . . They might be quite good.' So I think my point is that there's always a danger that if you write a piece of social satire, some people will take it as a recipe.

MR: Scary . . . one of the bits I love in *The Handmaid's Tale* is the Scrabble game. In the process of that Offred says 'Context is all'. Is that a kind of motto for you?

MA: I think it's probably a motto for human society. It's not an original thought of mine: anybody given to the study of anthropology or history, or even the history of fashion design, will tell you exactly the same thing. Simple example: this year's hot dress number is going to be very ancient in five years. But it might have been quite desirable at the time. You know, we do code everything as to whether it's the new and upcoming thing, or whether it was last year's thing, and we code many things in our lives in the same way that we code fashion.

MR: Code really intrigues you, doesn't it? Laws, systems of social behaviour, what's normal, what isn't normal?

MA: Well, let's go back to the Scrabble for a minute. Once something becomes forbidden, it also becomes potentially transgressive, and therefore it acquires an electrical charge. Under slavery in the United States it was legally forbidden for a slave to read or write; it was one of the things they didn't want them to do, because they might get ideas. And the regime in *The Handmaid's Tale* says, 'We won't make that mistake again' – i.e. letting women read.

MR: It also gives you a good game with words.

MA: Well, if it's forbidden, and suddenly there are these two people in a room and one of the people who shouldn't be doing it *is* doing it, then it acquires a sexual charge. The language itself – just the permission to use it, or the little window of opportunity to use it – becomes very appealing to her, and probably has a certain kinky attraction for him as well.

MR: The first section of *The Handmaid's Tale* ends of course with the girls, who are being trained by the Aunts, speaking to each other. The last line is their names – the names that will then be lost: 'Alma', 'Janine', 'Moira'. What does this question of naming mean to you?

MA: I think it is at the heart of the – shall we say – human experiment. We are the animal with syntax. We have the past tense, we have the future tense, we have the ability to put together subordinate clauses and qualifying phrases. So that seems to be at the centre of who we are. Language is therefore very important. And the *real name* of someone – their I, their ego – is very much attached to what kind of language they find themselves embedded within. It's in every child-raising book: don't tell your child, 'You are stupid'; say, 'That was a stupid thing to do.' In other words, do not attach that word 'stupid' to the child. Attach it to the act. In a way, you could say that each one of us is composing a narrative, composing 'the story of my life' at every stage of that life. That you are your narrative. If you read accounts of people who've completely lost their memories you realise how attached to our narratives we are, how much we define ourselves by them. It used to be that this was attached to the ancestral roll call – all the 'begats' in the Bible, or people who would write out their ancestry, with all of the various noble escutcheons, like dogs' pedigrees. You were not only the history of your own life, you were the history of all your ancestors' lives as well. I think it is deeply important. And to have your name taken away from you, and be assigned a number (which is what happened in the [Nazi-run concentration] camps), is a deeply depersonalising thing to do to someone.

MR: This question of composing not only your own narrative, but composing something that's behind, is a theme that's in the first story in *Bluebeard's Egg*, 'Significant Moments in the Life of My Mother'. Except, of course, it's not only the mother of the narrator, it's also the narrator, and the family of the mother of the narrator, all spilling out. As so often when reading your work, I feel as though I'm doing what happens within the story; doing the washing-up in the kitchen with the other women, and hearing these whispered stories or exchanges. How important to you is that whole business of storytelling to a particular audience?

MA: Again, this is not an original thought, but what is said has a lot to do not only with who is saying it, but with the audience to whom they are saying it. We do shape our stories according to our audience quite a bit. There are some things we will say to some people and other things we wouldn't dream of saying to those people, but we'll tell to somebody else. We will even change the story a little – and we change our own stories. For instance, a story that may have had a tragic form when you were twenty acquires a comic form when you're forty, and when you're eighty-five you may not be able to remember it at all. So our stories change. And it's partly because we, as our own audiences, change. Even the stories we tell to ourselves change, because we are actually telling them to a different person, or to a different form of that person.

There was once an academic who wrote a piece that said, 'It doesn't matter whether a story is written in the first, second or third person', and I could not disagree more. It's essential.

MR: When you start to write something, does it come to you cleanly as something that has be in the first or the third person?

MA: No, I have to know which person it's going to be in, and sometimes I start off in the wrong one. Then I reach a wall and I have to turn back, and find the right person. I usually have to know – if it's a first-person narrative – who that talking 'I' is addressing: to whom is the story being told? Is it somebody within the story? Or is it 'dear reader'? Is it the reader? Or is the reader a voyeur, watching the talking 'I' addressing another person within the story? Or is it, for instance, someone in the future – we don't even know who it might be yet?

There's a moment right at the beginning of [George Orwell's] *Nineteen Eighty-Four* where Winston Smith, the hero of that dire dystopia, is walking along the street and he sees an antique store, and in the antique store there's a beautiful journal with cream-coloured paper, and the pages are blank, and he feels he must have this, and he buys it, even though he knows it's a subversive thing to do. And then he buys some ink, because such paper needs to be written on with proper ink, and then he thinks, 'But to whom would I write?' Because he's living in a totalitarian society where self-expression is forbidden. 'Because if I write to anyone today, they won't be able to read me, and if I'm addressing the future, they won't be able to understand me.' So I think there's always that element of 'message in a bottle', thrown out into the sea . . . who will read it? In a second-person narrative – for instance, the epistolary novel made up of letters, a form that was so popular in the eighteenth century – we always knew to whom those letters were addressed; they were always addressed to specific people within the story. But when it's just an 'I' speaking, or even an author saying 'he' and 'she', it's less clear.

MR: Can you give me an example of an occasion when you actually changed the voice of the narrator?

MA: I started *Alias Grace* in the third person, and had to switch it to the first. I started *The Blind Assassin* three times. The first time I started in the third person, about an old lady who was dead. The narrating 'I' was a person who was still living, although it wasn't an 'I', it was a 'she', and she was cleaning up after this dead old lady. She found a container, which was a hatbox, and inside the container there were some letters. And that didn't work. Out it went.

I started again. This time the old lady was alive. She was being encountered by two other people, a 'he' and a 'she'. And she was being discovered through their encounters with her. She also had a container, she had a suitcase. And in the suitcase there was a photograph album. She had to go out of the window very quickly, because the 'he' and the 'she' started getting involved with each other and, worse than that, he was already married and had twins. So they're off in a bureau drawer somewhere, carrying on with their lives.

Then I started again. This time the old lady spoke for herself. And this is when the novel that we have with us today actually began, once she started speaking for herself. She too had a container. It was a steamer trunk, and inside the steamer trunk were the very things that are inside the steamer trunk today. There was always a container, there was always another level of narrative presented by what was in the container, and there was always an elderly lady. But as for the approach, how to get her to talk: usually the best way is to make her into an 'I' and let her speak for herself.

MR: The sense of a double perspective is something which threads through all of your work. I suppose it is these several narratives working against one another. How conscious are you of doing that?

MA: I'm fairly conscious. The simplest form of narrative is the picaresque as-it-happens adventure, you know, first this happens, then that happens, then that happens, then you can't do that, because there will never be a double perspective, there's only one line of time. If you think of it in terms of knitting, it's the plain stitch. If you think of it in terms of embroidery, it's the outline stitch. It's just the straightforward thing, no looping back, no overlaying, no seeing down through layers of time: there is only one timeline. And I long to write a book like that. I just have never done it.

MR: Your 'knitting' is very complicated.

MA: It's not that complicated. I probably grew up reading a bit too much Henry James. But the simple form of that narrative would be a book like [Robert Louis Stevenson's] *Treasure Island*. Even that has a map, even that has a past, even that is a story based on something that happened before, because of course nothing begins just out of nowhere. There's always something that has happened before what you're reading in the novel. But Stevenson had a way of filling those prior parts in fairly quickly, and then getting on with the present-time narrative.

MR: In a way, you memorialise exactly that process in *The Blind*

Assassin in the 'science-fiction' part of the story, when those monuments of stone are a deliberate act of both forgetting and remembering.

MA: That again comes right out of the Bible. You can find it in the section that follows the battle of Jericho. There is a town that is destroyed, and its name is 'Ai' – and that name means 'heap of rubble'. So obviously no town actually called itself 'heap of rubble', but whatever it really called itself is lost and gone for ever. So it's known by the name of its own destruction.

MR: And the name of its absence. Often when textbooks give a little summary of your work they say *The Handmaid's Tale* is odd, it's different from the others because it uses this science-fiction method. Of course *The Blind Assassin* also uses something like that.

MA: It incorporates a different kind of narrative. *The Handmaid's Tale* is speculative fiction. It's in the tradition of *Nineteen Eighty-Four* and [Aldous Huxley's] *Brave New World*, or indeed [Thomas More's] *Utopia*, to some extent. None of those traded in bug-eyed monsters, spaceships, other dimensions of time, technologies we don't have. None of those things are in any of those books. They all deal with human arrangements. And in *The Handmaid's Tale* I was very careful to have nothing that we hadn't already done, or for which we don't already have the technology. We could do it all, we have done it all. These are things that human beings do, given half a chance – alas!

By contrast, science-fiction fantasy, particularly as exemplified in the pulp science fiction of the Thirties, was all on other planets. It had bug-eyed monsters, it had lizard men, and the two-thousand-year-old undead women have a long pedigree. But they were very popular in those works. And those works were also stuffed with colour adjectives. Partly because the pulps themselves were not illustrated in colour. They had colour covers, but that kind of printing hadn't been perfected yet, so inside they were black and white, and everything is therefore 'azure' or 'sapphirine' – all of these very exotic descriptions. One feature is that the beautiful undead women are very fond of filmy garments. Anyway, that's another form. I wouldn't say that it's particularly serious social satire. The man telling this story, who writes for the pulps, is, however, building into it his own social satire, which is a commentary on the hierarchical arrangements and power politics of his time. Why was I interested in the Thirties? I think we're coming back to them.

MR: Coming back to the Thirties?

MA: Oh yes. I mean you had parts of society that were very rich. You had large segments that were poor, to the point of desperation. On a global scale, that's where we are now. You have some countries that are very rich, you have other countries that are very poor, to the point of desperation. You had a few people with lots of power, you had other people with no power. Look around you. And that all came boiling up in the social confrontations and divisions of the Thirties, finally culminating in the big explosion that was the Second World War. So I don't think this is a thing of the past.

MR: Freedom is related to that question. I was struck by one of the stories in *Bluebeard's Egg*, where there's a description of the society in which she lived which had these rigid parameters, but within which there was what you call 'an astonishing freedom'. What does freedom mean to you?

MA: Well, freedom is one of these words that is very important to us, but when we're asked to define it, we can't quite say what we think it means. But we can give lots of examples of what it isn't. And I feel that this is how dystopia works as a form. Books like *The Handmaid's Tale* are presumably examples of what we don't want to be. So, we may not know what we want to be, but we know what we don't want to be. We may not know what it is to love, but we know what it is to hate – because we've all gone to school, and had our interactions with our innocent little playmates.

I think the problem with defining heaven, which always comes up in a quite boring way, is that people have a lot more trouble formulating their image of the ideal than they do in formulating hell. We know quite a lot about hell, we've seen it put into practice several times in the past century. A lot of people are living in it right now. But what would heaven be? Would it be like a retirement villa? And if so, wouldn't we be bored? So that's the problem with freedom. Freedom as we experience it is always relative. People who like their jobs feel freer than people who don't like their jobs. But people who like their jobs still have jobs. They're still, in a sense, at the mercy of someone else, or some other system. People who are richer feel freer than people who are poorer. But they're still constrained by the existence of money. It could run out; they might want more. They're still caught up in some limiting system that says, 'You could be richer, you could be poorer.' How free do you feel within that system? Well, freer than I might feel if I were starving. But total freedom is a thing of the imagination. Total freedom is when we can fly without airplanes.

MR: There's a theme of falling in your work. *The Blind Assassin* begins with Laura . . .

MA: Oh, golly. You mean falling down . . . out of planes?

MR: Yes. Out of planes in *Cat's Eye*, off cliffs, the Gorge, Laura driving her car off a bridge . . .

MA: Yes. People also used to say, 'There seems to be a preoccupation with drowning.' If you go back far enough, there's that too. You only have a limited choice of ways of disposing of people. Suppose you want them out of the way in your narrative. Suppose you want them to have ceased to be alive in some fashion. They can die of a disease. They can be murdered. They can die in an accident. There actually aren't any other ways. Within accidents, there are: drowning, fires, hurricanes, water, fire, air, falling down holes, or falling off something. So you're limited to variations of those: earthquakes, thunderstorms.

MR: It's as practical as that? There's no element of risk?

MA: Well, you're always taking a risk when you do one of these things, because if you do it in an improbable way, people will think it is rubbish. It has to be appropriate to the landscape in which the characters find themselves. You're not going to have somebody dying from falling off a fourteen-storey building if they're in the middle of the desert and there aren't any buildings. There have to be the means at hand – apt means. And it has to be something that somebody could actually do, or that could actually happen to them. You'd be very unlikely to die of a tornado in Norway, unless the climate changes a lot. But it would be quite easy to die of one in Arkansas. They have a lot of them. So, it's what's available. And Toronto is full of ravines. It's full of ravines with bridges over them. Ravines and water. Unless you want somebody to die in a fire, those are pretty much the choices. There aren't a lot of tornadoes there. You might die in a hurricane – there have been some. But you would not die, often, in a hurricane.

MR: This is making your fiction sound very macabre.

MA: Let's put it this way. There's a chapter in *The Blind Assassin* called the 'Peach Women of A'Aa'. And in that, the narrator – who is the man telling the story to his beloved – deals with the question 'Why can't it be happier?' She says, 'Why can't it be happier?', and he says, 'You want it to be happy? All right, here we go.' And he tells a story in which two men end up in what seems at first to be Paradise. There's no death. Then what? Then what? Then they get bored. Then they try to get out. Then they find they can't get out. Then it becomes a prison. Then she says, 'You've got to let them out. You can't just leave them there.' And he says, 'Well, outside is death.'

Because the novel, as a form, is about time. I would say time, money and love are the three central subjects of the novel, with time and money being the constraints, and love being the thing that once in a while transcends them. But if you have time, you also have, eventually, death. Because time moves on. You can't avoid it. Some people in a novel – if it's a novel of any length – will die.

MR: *The Blind Assassin* brings together so many things that you've used before, or done before. Is it the end of a cycle?

MA: It may be the end of a cycle. At this time I don't know whether it's the end of a cycle, the beginning of a cycle or something off to the side. And it's easy to see, or it's easy to say, that certain motifs come up in the work of this or that writer, but on the other hand aren't they the motifs that come up in the novel as a form, quite repeatedly? Time, love and money, and various arrangements of those things.

That's if it's a novel. By which I mean, if it is actually dealing with society, as opposed to a romance, which is a little bit off to the side. The actual functionings of society don't concern romance as much.

MR: In *The Blind Assassin* Laura Chase's book – which is the novel within the novel, 'The Blind Assassin' – is reviled and gets banned. Of course, this has been happening to *The Handmaid's Tale*. What's the latest stage with this? What's going on in Texas [where some parents objected to their children reading the book on school courses]? And how do you feel about that?

MA: Well, this isn't the first time. It's been banned quite a lot. I'm in good company. And on the one hand you have to say, 'We cannot have a society in which parents are allowed no say in what their children read at school.' You know that would be another form of totalitarianism. And on the other hand we can also say, 'Nothing increases book sales more than to get yourself banned somewhere.' I think it's a bit absurd, that if this is the idea of titillating sex, I would say that these people have led somewhat constrained lives and have somewhat curious ideas, but you cannot determine people's reactions to your books. If it's a book with any power, there's always going to be some form of uproar.

My secret is that, in the Western zodiac, I'm a Scorpio. But, in the Eastern zodiac, I'm only a rabbit. So what you have to picture is someone who essentially wants a quiet life, but if you put your foot down its rabbit hole, you might get a nasty bite.

VINTAGE
LIVING
TEXTS

The Handmaid's Tale

IN CLOSE-UP

Reading guides for

THE HANDMAID'S TALE

BEFORE YOU BEGIN TO READ . . .
— Read the interview with Atwood. You will see that she identifies there a number of themes and techniques that are discussed in *The Handmaid's Tale*. These include:

- Narrative structure
- History
- Political manipulation and moral choice
- Time and memory
- Naming
- Addresser, address, addressee
- Utopia and dystopia.

Other themes that it may be useful to consider while reading the novel include:

- Relations between men and women
- Absence and presence.

While you are reading *The Handmaid's Tale*, *Bluebeard's Egg* and *The Blind Assassin* in detail it is worth bearing the overall themes listed at the beginning of each reading guide in mind. At the end of each reading guide you will find suggested contexts, which will help you to situate the novels' themes in a wider framework. The reading activities given below are not designed to be followed slavishly. Choose whichever most interest you or are most useful for your own purposes. The questions that are set at intervals are to help you relate parts of the novel to the whole.

Reading activities: detailed analysis

EPIGRAPHS

Focus on: reference and allusion

CONSIDER . . .

— Read each of the three epigraphs to the novel. Jot down the thoughts that come to you as you read. What sort of book do these quotations make you imagine that you will be reading? Keep your notes: you will need them later.

— Look at Atwood's novel *The Blind Assassin* (2001). It also has three quotations functioning as epigraphs. Read those, and make notes again. You might find that some of her concerns in the two different novels are along the same lines.

SECTION HEADINGS

Focus on: expectation and the reversal of expectation

STATE . . .

— Look at the fifteen section headings for *The Handmaid's Tale*. What do they make you think of? Setting aside odd terms like 'Soul Scrolls', 'Jezebel's' and 'Salvaging', what do these section headings suggest to you? If we added in 'Nappy Change', would it be out of place? What does this suggest about the way in which the reader's expectations are being manipulated and challenged?

SECTION I. NIGHT.
CHAPTER 1 (pp. 13–14)

Focus on: irony and ironic juxtapositions

ASK YOURSELF . . .
— Where are we? Section I is called 'Night'. This chapter begins with the words 'We slept . . .' It ends (second from last line) '. . . from bed to bed'. How do we know that what we are being offered is not a lullaby or a bedtime story? Write out the words that comfort and reassure. Write out the words that challenge and shock. Look particularly at the page turn from p. 13 to 14: 'Aunt Sara and Aunt Elizabeth patrolled; they had electric cattle prods slung on thongs from their leather belts.' Why is the change of tone here so shocking? Look at the information given to us on p. 13 and compare it with what goes on on p. 14. In what ways are your reactions as a reader being manipulated?

COMPARE . . .
— *The Handmaid's Tale* has been compared to George Orwell's dystopian fiction *Nineteen Eighty-Four* (1949). Atwood herself makes the same comparison in the interview. Read the first chapter of *Nineteen Eighty-Four*. What methods does Orwell use to make us realise that this is a different world with very different rules and expectations? How does Orwell's method compare with Atwood's? In what ways is it the same? In what ways is it different?

SECTION II. SHOPPING.
CHAPTER 2 (pp. 17–21)

Focus on: word play

IDENTIFY . . .

— Consider these phrases: 'Waste not, want not. I am not being wasted. What do I want?' (p. 17). And 'for ladies in reduced circumstances. That is what we are now. The circumstances have been reduced; for those of us who still have circumstances' (p. 18). In each of these cases Atwood has taken a cliché and made it 'alive' again. She plays with it for many meanings. Find other examples of this technique with vocabulary in this chapter, and look for others as you read the novel as a whole. We will come back to this question, but remember the ways that language is used and abused in the setting of the novel, and be conscious of this issue at all times during your reading.

Focus on: narrative and social exchange

COMPARE . . .

— Read the first story, 'Significant Moments in the Life of My Mother', in Atwood's collection of short stories called *Bluebeard's Egg*. Compare the social setting for the telling of stories and the exchange of a solidarity of experience, as set out in that story, with the episode here where Offred hears Rita and Cora talking in the kitchen (pp. 20–1). In what ways are similar themes and concepts being set up in the story and in this scene in the novel?

SECTION II
CHAPTER 3 (pp. 22–6)

Focus on: characterisation

CONSIDER . . .

— In the encounters described between the Commander's wife and Offred, both Offred and we are learning about the wife at the same time. Offred realises at the end of this chapter that the wife is Serena Joy, an erstwhile religious-revivalist television star. Analyse the way in which Serena Joy's character is built up for us through Offred's perspective.

SECTION II
CHAPTERS 4, 5 AND 6 (pp. 27–43)

Focus on: setting and estrangement

LIST AND ANALYSE . . .

— This section is headed with the innocuous title 'Shopping'. But in the course of Offred's journey and her conversations with Ofglen we are given a number of pieces of information that make us realise that this scene is not as straightforward as it appears to be. Where are we? What are the rules of behaviour? What are the penalties for not conforming? List as many examples of the unexpected as you can from these chapters. Write down also why they surprise or challenge you. Outline the ways in which the ordinary is challenged by the extraordinary.

SECTION III. NIGHT.
CHAPTER 7 (pp. 47–50)

Focus on: the theme of storytelling

EXAMINE AND EVALUATE . . .

— Offred gives us three scenes from her past, framed by two from her present. She is anxious about the story she is telling, and to whom she is telling it. '*Dear You*, I'll say. Just you, without a name' (p. 49). Look at the interview with Atwood where she speaks about the importance for a novelist of knowing who is speaking and to whom.

— Assess Offred's situation in the light of her memories here. How far is the storytelling drive taking over the story? Ask yourself also some practical questions. Is Offred writing this down? If so, with what? Is she telling it to herself in her head? If so, where has the story that we are reading come from? We will come back to these questions later.

SECTION IV. WAITING ROOM.
CHAPTERS 8, 9, 10, 11 AND 12 (pp. 53–76)

Focus on: vocabulary, word choice and suggestion

SEARCH FOR . . .

— At the beginning of this section Offred thinks about words. The distress signal 'Mayday', which comes from the French '*M'aidez*' ('Help me') for instance. She also thinks about Serena Joy's name, and about Aunt Lydia's misquotation from the Bible, which she corrects in her head (p. 55). Look through all the chapters in this section and note down the instances where words are examined, explained, analysed or misused. Why – in this particular political and social situation – is the use and abuse of language so important? Note that the regime under which Offred lives makes up many neologisms, or new words, and 'invents' old names for new concepts and terms – Econowives, Marthas, Salvaging, Guardians.

CONSIDER . . .
— On p. 57 Offred says, 'I would like to have a knife like that.' Analyse this sentence. It is very simple grammatically. But what does it say in this context? Why would Offred like to have such a knife?

Focus on: names

ASK YOURSELF . . .
— Why is Offred called Offred? And Ofglen? And Ofwarren? If you look at the interview with Atwood you will see that she has something to say there about names and the importance of naming. If you look forward to p. 94 in *The Handmaid's Tale* you will see that Offred thinks about her name – or her names, including her old name (which we never learn).

Looking over Sections I to IV

QUESTIONS FOR DISCUSSION OR ESSAYS
1. 'I compose myself. Myself is a thing I must now compose, as one composes a speech' (p. 76). Consider how this statement is borne out by the character of Offred's narrative so far.

2. 'Freedom from' or 'freedom to': how are these two different kinds of 'freedom' perceived in the world of *The Handmaid's Tale*?

3. Analyse the layering of time in the first sections of *The Handmaid's Tale*.

4. '*The Handmaid's Tale* is a realist text set in a fantasy world.' Discuss.

SECTION V. NAP.
CHAPTER 13 (pp. 79–85)

Focus on: characterisation

DESCRIBE AND DEFINE . . .

— Offred thinks about herself: 'I used to think well of myself. I didn't then' (p. 82). How does this chapter contribute to Offred's characterisation? Consider her ideas about her body – as she once was and as she is now. Consider also her relationship to Moira, and to Luke and to her lost little girl. Note that Luke and her child only appear in 'dreams' – if, of course, they are dreams.

SECTION VI. HOUSEHOLD.
CHAPTERS 14, 15, 16 AND 17 (pp. 89–110)

Focus on: realism and representation

CRITICALLY EVALUATE . . .

— The chapters in this section are packed with descriptive details of furniture, clothes, smells, bodies. These are 'realist' descriptions, much in the manner of a nineteenth-century novel where you will be told what characters are wearing and what their furniture is like. Look up the word 'realist' in the glossary of literary terms.

But the text itself in *The Handmaid's Tale* is not 'realist'. It moves from a present tense to past memories; it includes dreams and speculations on the part of the first-person narrator. Offred's thoughts are sometimes relayed as they come to her, and sometimes recorded as if she is making a testimony of her experience. This is an adaptation of a narrative method that is generally called 'stream of consciousness'. Look up that term also. In what ways might you argue that Offred's narrative is, in fact, 'realist'?

ILLUSTRATE . . .
— In Chapter 15 several strands of narrative are interwoven. We see the scene in Serena Joy's parlour, we hear the Commander reading from the Bible, and we are given Offred's memories of Moira. Illustrate how each of these three elements is represented, and consider how they round out the whole picture that you have in your mind. How far would you describe this scene, or scenes, as 'real'?

CONSIDER AND EXPLAIN . . .
— Read Chapter 16. What is going on here is very strange and yet very familiar. Analyse the ways in which the narrative creates a sense of estrangement, makes the ordinary into the unfamiliar, the 'real' into the surreal.

Focus on: rebellion and context

TRACE . . .
— Look over Chapter 17. In what ways does Offred assert herself? Are they large or small gestures? If you did any of these things, would they be rebellious? Consider how they become so in the context of Offred's life and situation.

SECTION VII. NIGHT.
CHAPTER 18 (pp. 113–16)

Focus on: narrative structure

COMPARE . . .
— Look back at Sections I, III and V and compare them with
this section. Three of these sections are called 'Night', and one
is called 'Nap'. Each consists of just one short chapter. But
what else links these passages? Write out a list of what happens in each and compare the information you are given there.
How do these short sections structure the narrative? How much
would you lose if they weren't there? Note that there are four
more sections called 'Night' coming up at IX, XI, XIII and
XV. Keep your notes and add to them when you get to those
sections.

SECTION VIII. BIRTH DAY.
CHAPTERS 19, 20, 21, 22 AND 23 (pp. 119–50)

Focus on: connections

ACCOUNT FOR . . .
— This section is entitled 'Birth Day'. Count up how many
births we are told about here. Include both actual births (like
that of Ofwarren's daughter), Offred's memory of the birth
of her daughter, and Offred's memories of her mother and
her own birth. Count also as many metaphorical 'births' as you
can find: Moira's escape from the Centre, for instance. How
do all of these births – real and imagined – connect together
to make a pattern of reference and implication?

RELATE . . .

— In Chapter 23 the Commander asks Offred to play Scrabble with him. Relate this passage to other passages in the novel as a whole where the question of the manipulation of words, of pejorative or valorised language, or of access to literacy is discussed.

RETELL . . .

— Look at the words that the Commander and Offred create in their game of Scrabble: Larynx, Valance, Quince, Zygote, Limp, Gorge (p. 149). Write a story with as few sentences as possible, but it must include those words. What sort of story do you end up with? What kind of subtext is being suggested by these words?

Focus on: characterisation

INVENT AND RESTATE . . .

— As this is a first-person narrative we learn a great deal about Offred. But other characters are beginning to come into view as well. Write a short description of Janine, Moira and Offred's mother. How much have you learned about each of them so far? In what ways, in the light of her attitudes to each of them, do they help to define Offred's character?

Looking over Sections V to VIII

QUESTIONS FOR DISCUSSION OR ESSAYS

1. 'This is a reconstruction' (p. 144). In what ways might the whole of *The Handmaid's Tale* be considered 'a reconstruction'?

2. 'There's nothing in this book that hasn't already happened or isn't happening elsewhere' (Atwood). Discuss.

SECTION IX. NIGHT.
CHAPTER 24 (pp. 153–6)

Focus on: self-creation and self-deception

COMPARE . . .

— Offred realises that this is a turning point in her own story. Work out how she thinks about herself and her choices at this moment. Then she remembers seeing an old film about the mistress of a Nazi leader. She thinks about how this woman also constructed a sense of self. Compare and contrast Offred's self-creation – or self-deception – with that of the mistress.

SECTION X. SOUL SCROLLS.
CHAPTERS 25, 26, 27, 28 AND 29 (pp. 159–98)

Focus on: images and figurative language

CONNECT AND EVALUATE . . .

— Look for places in this section where images and words that you have already seen are beginning to be repeated to make a pattern. For instance, on p. 161 Offred says, 'What I coveted was the shears.' Look back to the place where she coveted a knife, and put the implications of the two together. Later on she will tell the Commander that 'they' search her room for razor blades.

— Alternatively, look at the passage on pp. 161–2 where Offred contemplates the burgeoning garden, the plants and the flowers quick with life. Find other such passages. How do they relate – figuratively – to the subject matter and the concerns of the novel as a whole?

— Or look at p. 164. The Commander and Offred play another game of Scrabble. Again, write a story using the words that we are told they manage to spell. What kind of a story is this? How might you relate these images to the story in, or the method of, the novel as a whole? Later on (p. 193) Offred spells 'Zilch'. You might add that to your story.

— Or look at the passage on pp. 195–7 where Offred asks the Commander about the Latin phrase she has found written inside the cupboard in her room. Think about all the things you know about this sentence now. What does it mean to the Commander? What does it mean to Offred? What did it mean to the Handmaid who wrote it? How do their three different attitudes compare?

Focus on: the theme of men and women

COMPARE AND CONTRAST . . .

— On p. 172 Offred says, 'The fact is that I'm his mistress.' Why does she think of herself as the Commander's mistress now, as opposed to earlier on in the story? What has changed?

— Now look at p. 191 after Offred has related the stories of how her credit card was cancelled and how she was fired from her job. Luke wanted to make love; she didn't. Why not? Offred remembers that she realised Luke didn't really mind about the things that were happening to her, and to women in general. And this was even at a time before the establishment of the Gilead regime – that is, when attitudes to women at large were still supposed to be liberal, just as they are (supposed to be) in Western society today. Make a comparison between Luke and the Commander. In what ways might you make an argument for their attitudes to women being much the same?

SECTION XI. NIGHT.
CHAPTER 30 (pp. 201–5)

Focus on: addresser, address and addressee

RESEARCH AND COMPARE . . .

— Offred prays in this section. She prays to God, but she has to invent that 'You'. Search for some prayers. What is the point of a prayer? Is it a speech to someone else? If so, to whom? Is it more about the addresser – the one doing the speaking? Or is it more about the addressee – the one to whom the prayer is addressed? How do you know that a passage of text, or a spoken speech, is a prayer? What form of address does it take? What rhetorical patterns might be used?

— At the beginning of Alice Walker's *The Color Purple* (1982), Celie, the heroine, writes a letter to God. Compare her style of 'prayer' to that used in this section.

Focus on: the theme of living and dying

INTERPRET . . .

— Offred remembers how Luke killed their pet cat before they made their attempt to escape. She ends this section with a question: 'How can I keep on living?' (p. 205). Interpret the many meanings of 'living', 'dying' and 'killing' in the novel so far.

SECTION XII. JEZEBEL'S.
CHAPTERS 31, 32, 33, 34, 35, 36, 37, 38 AND 39
(pp. 209–67)

Focus on: characterisation

ANALYSE AND COMMENT ON . . .
— Chapters 31, 32 and 33 offer more detailed information about some of the other characters in Offred's present orbit, as well as in her memory. These include (from Offred's present) Ofglen, Serena Joy, Rita and Janine, and (from Offred's past) Janine, Moira and Offred's mother. Choose two of these characters and write down six key words that describe them. Are they words that are in the text? Or are they words that come to you as you think about their characters? Comment on how Offred's highly restricted social world is being expanded by her changing relations with Serena Joy, Rita and Ofglen.

OUTLINE AND RETELL . . .
— On pp. 212–13 and 214 Offred thinks briefly about her mother. Look through the book so far and jot down every time Offred's mother is referred to or described. Then write a description of her character using the information you have gleaned from these sections.

Focus on: history and perspective

TRACE AND EXPLAIN . . .
During their illicit Scrabble meetings the Commander explains to Offred the principles of the regime in Gilead and how it is that the present situation is an improvement on the social arrangement that went before. The account of this episode begins on pp. 220–2 while Offred is lying in her room pretending to nap, and it resumes on pp. 231–2 as Offred recalls the conversation while she is at the Prayvaganza. What he is

describing as the past – in the world of the novel – is effectively an account of a time close to our time now. All these things obtained in the Western world of the late twentieth century and are still recognisable in the early twenty-first century.
— The Commander gives a skewed political perspective, but how many of his criticisms of the recent past might you agree with? We know that Offred feels nostalgic for that past, but might there be anything that convinces you of the accuracy of his criticisms in his version?

TO WHAT EXTENT? . . .
— What is the dramatic effect of splitting Offred's memory of this conversation and scattering her recollections through her descriptions of where she is and what is happening? How far does this narrative method contribute to our sense of an argument being carried out on the theme of 'freedom to' versus 'freedom from'? Are you convinced by Offred's response when she tells the Commander (pp. 231–2) that what they left out was 'love'? What do you think she means?

Focus on: language, vocabulary choice and style

CRITICALLY EVALUATE . . .
— Read the opening paragraph of Chapter 35 (p. 236). Consider how the word 'space' is used and defined within the text here. Then consider also the play on the words 'invalid', 'valid' and 'invalidated'. Look up each of these three words in a dictionary. Evaluate the effects of Offred's own textual analysis here. Is it partly word play, partly punning, partly teasing out definitions?
— First of all, analyse this technique in relation to the fictional narrator. Why is it relevant that Offred thinks in this way? In what ways is it appropriate to her situation and character?

45

— Then consider the fact that Atwood is the author of this text and that she is also a prominent writer of poetry. What poetic results are achieved by letting words mean more than one thing at once?

— Look then at the section on pp. 237–9 where Offred goes back again to the conversation with the Commander about love. Count up the number of times that similar techniques using puns, word play and definitions are used.

Focus on: allusion

SEARCH . . .

— The 'club' to which the Commander takes Offred is called 'Jezebel's'. Look up the name of Jezebel in a concordance to the Bible or in a *Bible Companion*. Then read the relevant section. How does the original story relate to what is going on in these scenes in *The Handmaid's Tale*?

Focus on: scene setting, mood and point of view

SEARCH AND COMPARE . . .

— On p. 246 Offred recognises the club to which the Commander has taken her as an hotel that she had visited with Luke. Compare the descriptions of the hotel as it is now with what it once was. Look ahead to Chapter 39 for more descriptions. And look back at the opening section of Chapter 9 (pp. 60–1) where Offred remembers visiting hotels with Luke. Contrast and compare her memories of these kinds of settings with her present. Consider the ironies in the contrast.

Focus on: narrative style

DISTINGUISH AND EXAMINE . . .

— On p. 256 Offred's narrative tells us 'I've tried to make it sound as much like her as I can. It's a way of keeping her alive.' These passages, where Offred meets up with Moira at Jezebel's, are the first time that we have read about Moira in person – other than in Offred's memory. Consider the ways in which Offred attempts to invoke Moira's character and style of talking. Underline appropriate words and phrases that contribute to this language-based picture of Moira.

Looking over Sections IX to XII

QUESTIONS FOR DISCUSSION OR ESSAYS

1. 'But people will do anything rather than admit that their lives have no meaning. No use, that is. No plot' (p. 227). Consider the concerns and the methods of Offred's narrative in the light of this quotation.

2. '*The Handmaid's Tale* is our own tale.' Discuss.

3. Analyse the different attitudes to men and women displayed by the Commander and by Offred.

4. Discuss the images and idea of heroism in this section.

SECTION XIII. NIGHT.
CHAPTER 40 (pp. 271–5)

Focus on: narrative structure

OUTLINE . . .
— This is the penultimate 'Night' section and the first where Offred is – in terms of the present-tense narrative – not just confined to her own room in the Commander's house. Consider the ways in which this section differs from the previous 'Night' sections and outline the effects of this change of pattern.

EVALUATE . . .

— Several times in this chapter Offred tells us that she has made something up, and gives a revised version of her story instead. Is Offred a 'reliable' narrator, or not? What implications follow for how we read the text?

SECTION XIV. SALVAGING.
CHAPTERS 41, 42, 43, 44 AND 45 (pp. 279–99)

Focus on: narrative structure

EXPLAIN . . .

— Offred says that she wishes the story were different (p. 279). She says that it is a story in 'fragments, like a body caught in crossfire or pulled apart by force'. Consider the ways in which Offred's narrative – overall – is indeed 'fragmentary'. Then consider why it is that these two particular similes are appropriate and relevant images here. You should look back over the text for the 'body caught in crossfire', and forward for the body 'pulled apart by force'.

Focus on: addresser, address, addressee

ACCOUNT FOR . . .

— Offred's narrative spends some time working out who it is that she addresses and in what context she imagines the person addressed might be able to read (or, as it turns out, hear) her narrative. At this point (p. 279) the focus of her address seems to change. Might you be able to account for the fact that now the imagined person she addresses seems to be more 'real'? Who might her imagined audience be? And why has she suddenly started talking to that particular person?

Focus on: the theme of moral responsibility

ASK YOURSELF . . .

— What do you think of Ofglen's action on pp. 291–2? How does her choice relate to the theme of moral responsibility in the novel as a whole?

SECTION XV. NIGHT.
CHAPTER 46 (pp. 303–7)

Focus on: narrative structure and conclusions

REVISE AND EXPLAIN . . .

— Several paragraphs here begin with the words 'I could'. Much of the whole of Offred's narrative has been about possibilities rather than facts. On the other hand, many of the themes, phrases and images in this chapter refer back to episodes or thoughts that we have already been told about or heard: the knife and the garden shears, for instance; or the Latin tag in Offred's cupboard; or Serena Joy, the Commander, Nick. Assess the impact of this brief recapitulation of the main strands in the novel. And set them against the possibilities of escape that are now, or have been, open to Offred.

— On p. 307 Offred's narrative concludes with the words: 'And so I step up, into the darkness within; or else the light.' What do you think has happened? What is it in the text that makes you think that?

Focus on: the theme of naming

INTERPRET . . .

— When Nick is trying to convince Offred that she should go with these men who appear with the black van, he uses her

49

real name (p. 305). We never learn Offred's real name. Why not, do you think?

Looking over Sections XIII–XV

QUESTIONS FOR DISCUSSION OR ESSAYS

1. The writer Angela Carter described *The Handmaid's Tale* as 'both a superlative exercise in science fiction and a profoundly felt moral story'. In the light of your reading of the events of Section XIV, which would you consider the more appropriate description?

2. Analyse the significance of the fragmentary character of the narrative in Section XIV.

3. 'More rooms mean more possibilities. Which is why the narrative has to close'. Discuss, in relation to Sections XIII–XV of *The Handmaid's Tale*.

4. Which do you trust . . . the teller or the tale?

5. Consider the significance of images to do with light and dark in these sections.

6. In what ways does Offred buy new freedom in these last sections of the novel?

HISTORICAL NOTES ON
THE HANDMAID'S TALE
SECTION 1 (p. 311)
TRANSCRIPT HEADING

Focus on: tone and style

EXAMINE AND ASSESS . . .

— Read the heading that describes the supposed occasion taking place here. Why does it begin with a present participle, 'Being'? What kind of 'official' language or discourse is being used here?

— What do you make of the names of the two academics mentioned in this passage? Why 'Crescent Moon'? Why 'Darcy'? If you have read Jane Austen's novel *Pride and Prejudice* (1813) you will know that the protagonist is called Mr Darcy. What might this choice suggest about his namesake's character? And what about 'Pieixoto'? Further down (p. 311) you will see that 'Professor Johnny Running Dog' is mentioned. What does his name contribute? What kind of future society might be being hinted at in these names and in the descriptions of the two professors' posts?

HISTORICAL NOTES
SECTION 2 (pp. 311–12)
PROFESSOR CRESCENT MOON'S INTRODUCTION

Focus on: genre

CONSIDER THE GENRE AND LIST . . .

— Professor Crescent Moon's introduction is designed to welcome delegates to this lecture at an international conference, to make housekeeping announcements for the participants and to introduce the speaker whose lecture follows. It is a particular academic forum that is being portrayed here, but – given that this is fiction, and not a genuine transcript of a real event – what can you say about the genre adopted here? Which term would you give to it? Choose from the following:

- Comedy
- Satire
- Melodrama
- Parody
- Romance
- Epic
- Fable
- Irony.

— Look up these words in the glossary of literary terms if you are not familiar with them. When you have made your choice, list the phrases and terms in Crescent Moon's speech that bear out and support your selection.

Focus on: the theme of reading and interpretation

LIST, RESEARCH AND DESCRIBE . . .
— Pick out each of the titles of the papers and published works that Crescent Moon mentions (there are five in all). Then look back over the novel as a whole. What do the titles of these academic papers suggest about the book you have read? How do they relate to the circumstances that are portrayed in Offred's narrative? What more do these titles contribute to your understanding of the political and cultural situation in Gilead?

It will help you to look up the significance of Krishna and Kali; the Nazi policy on the Jewish ghettos during the Second World War; the workings of medieval sumptuary laws (that is, who was allowed to wear what, depending on class and status – you will find more about this in the contexts section); and the events that took place in Iran during the 1970s and 1980s. You might also like to consult the interview with Atwood. There is a section near the beginning where she speaks of how everything that takes place in *The Handmaid's Tale* has either happened or is happening in the world.

— With reference to the novel as a whole, why is the title of Professor Pieixoto's own talk ironic?

HISTORICAL NOTES
SECTION 3 (pp. 312–24)
PROFESSOR PIEIXOTO'S LECTURE

Focus on: jokes and vocabulary

RESEARCH AND ASSESS . . .
In his first three paragraphs (pp. 312–13) Professor Pieixoto makes several jokes based on puns, reference or word play: these include the joke about 'enjoy', the allusion to Chaucer, the pun on 'tail' and 'tale', and the similarity through assonance of 'Femaleroad' and 'Frailroad'.
— If you don't immediately understand these references, look them up, think about them or ask someone else. Then assess the impact and relevance of these jokes. What tone do they set up? How seriously can we take what is to come? What character is the speaker given in the light of his jokes? What is your own attitude towards him?

Focus on: the theme of narratives and storytelling

RESEARCH . . .
— We are now told that 'The Handmaid's Tale' has been given

that name in homage to Chaucer's *The Canterbury Tales* (begun 1387). How many other titles can you find that are called 'The ——'s Tale'? What sorts of stories are these? How might the use of this reference illuminate your reactions to the novel as a whole?

COMPARE AND EVALUATE . . .

— Pieixoto tells us (p. 313) that there are other examples of records like Offred's. Look for similar memoirs, whether fact or fiction. You might try *The Diary of Anne Frank* (1947) or Doris Lessing's novel *Memoirs of a Survivor* (1975). How do these books compare with *The Handmaid's Tale*? In what ways does Atwood's novel exploit similar techniques? In what ways are these narratives the same? In what ways are they different?

— We now discover that the narrative we have read is actually a transcript of tape recordings – something we did not know at the time, and could not guess at. In 2001 BBC Radio 4 broadcast a dramatisation of *The Handmaid's Tale* recorded 'on location' in Harvard, Massachusetts. This dramatisation was presented as if it were a tape recording – you heard the machine being switched on and off as Offred spoke her testimony into the microphone. What difference might it have made to your idea of the text if you had known all along that it was a tape recording?

— We also learn (p. 314) that Pieixoto and Wade have arranged the blocks of speech in an order that they consider appropriate. But that process of ordering is also an act of editing and interpreting. How does this revelation relate to the themes of the novel as a whole?

Focus on: the theme of 'freedom from' and 'freedom to'

CONSIDER . . .

— On pp. 314–15 Pieixoto proposes that his society 'must be

cautious about passing moral judgements'. Must we? Is morality always 'culture-specific'? Are there any crimes or behaviours that are always intolerable? Are there any that could be tolerated in extreme circumstances – in time of war, for instance – that could not be countenanced in periods of peace? How does *The Handmaid's Tale* open and deal with this question?

RESEARCH . . .
—— On pp. 316–17 Pieixoto lists the technical reasons for a declining birth rate in this fictional late twentieth century: his list includes the rise in the number of cases of sexually transmitted infections; nuclear-plant accidents; leakages from sites storing chemical and biological weapons of war; the routine use of chemicals, insecticide and herbicide sprays in farming technology. Research any of these – still current – topics. In what ways does each of these practices present a moral dilemma that can be labelled 'freedom from, versus freedom to'? For instance, how does 'freedom to' have lots of sex square with 'freedom from' the threat of infection? And how does humanity's need to live in a situation where we have 'freedom from' hunger square with an individual's 'freedom to' live in a rural environment that is not contaminated with chemicals?
—— We discover here that Canada was the 'safe' place beyond the borders of Gilead to which the condemned and persecuted wished to flee. Within the 'freedom from and freedom to' context that is worked out in the novel as a whole, research and consider the joke that makes Canada a happy alternative to America.

Focus on: the theme of the subordination of women

IDENTIFY AND DESCRIBE . . .
The academic researchers in this story decide here that it is important to identify the speaker in the tapes which they have

isolated and studied. They begin their trawl with the physical environment: where the tapes have come from, and the town that this place was at the time when the tapes were recorded. But they draw a blank. So Pieixoto and Wade then declare that they cannot get straight at the handmaid's tale: 'We held out no hope of tracing the narrator herself directly.' They can, so they conclude, only begin to identify 'Offred' indirectly: either in terms of her relationships with men (whether the Commander – is he Judd or Waterford? [p. 318–22]) or her relationship with Nick (might he have been a functionary within the underground organisation known as Mayday' [p. 322]?).

Obviously this future society inhabited by Professor Crescent Moon and Pieixoto *et al.* has a superior take on the past. They believe that they do not share, or could not tolerate, the social restrictions that obtained in twentieth-century Gilead.

— In your opinion, are their own perceptions of themselves accurate? Identify those signs that suggest their own sexism, racism or blinkered assumptions, and describe how those unacknowledged ideologies are skewing their own world picture.

— Look at Pieixoto's remarks on p. 322 about Offred's inadequacy as a narrator, 'had she had a different turn of mind' he says, 'She could have told us much about the workings of the Gileadean empire, had she had the instincts of a reporter or a spy.' What do you make of this?

CONSIDER AND ASSESS . . .

— Look at p. 320 where the hierarchy among women that held sway in Gilead is described. Look also at p. 321 where it is explained how the 'Aunts' got their names. What do you make of these two techniques of political expediency and propaganda? Describe how they are meant to work and consider whether or not you believe that they might.

Focus on: the theme of the significance of words and reading

REVISE, ANALYSE AND CONSIDER . . .

Waterford is credited with the invention of the terms 'Particicution' and 'Salvaging', though the practices themselves are shown to have been derived from older customs in other societies. The giving of fancy names to cruel rituals softens and orders the shock value that comes from realising what these things actually mean. How words can be used to disguise or distort reality is one of Atwood's themes in *The Handmaid's Tale*. The rulers in Gilead knew the power of words, which is why signs are pictorial rather than lettered. On p. 320 Judd – one of the candidates for the role of 'the Commander' in Offred's narrative – is said to have been credited with the remark 'Our big mistake was teaching them to read. We won't do that again.'

— Look back at the sections where Offred plays Scrabble with the Commander, in Chapters 23 (pp. 148–50), 25 (pp. 163–6) and 29 (pp. 193–8). Compare what we learn here about the manipulation of words and reading in Gilead with what goes on between Offred and the Commander. Then find other places in the novel where words – especially the coining or distorting of words – is made a key theme.

Focus on: allusions and reference

RESEARCH . . .

— Look up the story of Eurydice in a *Dictionary of Classical Mythology*. The Professor's remarks are part of his light-hearted wrapping-up speech. But consider seriously the implications of Eurydice's story and work out how they might apply to *The Handmaid's Tale* as a whole.

Focus on: endings

COMPARE . . .

— A film was made of *The Handmaid's Tale* in 1998. In that version the last shots we see of Offred show her living in a caravan in the woods and heavily pregnant. Which ending do you prefer: the film's or the conclusion in the novel? Why?

ANALYSE . . .

The last words of *The Handmaid's Tale* are:

> *Applause.*
> Are there any questions?

— Analyse the effect of this ending. Consider: a) what it means in the context of the conference; b) what it means in the context of Offred's narrative; and c) what it may mean in relation to your reading of the novel as a whole.

Looking over the Historical Notes and over the novel as a whole

QUESTIONS FOR DISCUSSION OR ESSAYS

1. 'Problems of Authentication in Reference to *The Handmaid's Tale*' is the title of Professor Pieixoto's talk. Analyse the ways in which the narrative methods of the novel ask questions about 'authority' and 'authentication'.

2. 'And so I step up, into the darkness within; or else the light.'

'Are there any questions?'

Assess why either or both of these two last lines are appropriate to the themes worked out in *The Handmaid's Tale*.

3. In what ways does your attitude change: a) to Offred and

b) to the narrative you have read, in the light of the 'Historical Notes'?

4.   'History is always a misrepresentation. Only personal testimony is true.'

'A first-person narrator is always an unreliable narrator.'

Discuss either or both of these remarks in relation to *The Handmaid's Tale*.

5.   Consider the proposition that the 'Historical Notes' – far from being objective – display sexist assumptions as blatant as those that are endorsed in Gilead.

6.   Consider the roles of allusion and reference (to texts, to historical events, to art works, to games) in *The Handmaid's Tale*.

7.   The third epigraph to *The Handmaid's Tale* reads: '"In the desert there is no sign that says, Thou shalt not eat stones" – Sufi proverb.' Now that you have read the whole book, discuss how this epigraph relates to the themes of the novel as a whole.

Contexts, comparisons and complementary readings

THE HANDMAID'S TALE

These sections suggest contextual and comparative ways of reading these three novels by Atwood. You can put your reading in a social, historical or literary context. You can make comparisons – again, social, literary or historical – with other texts or art works. Or you can choose complementary works (of whatever kind) – that is, art works, literary works, social reportage or facts that in some way illuminate the text by sidelights or interventions which you can make into a telling framework. Some of the suggested contexts are directly connected to the book, in that they will give you precise literary or social frames in which to situate the novel. In turn, these are either related to the period within which the novel is set or to the time – now – when you are reading it. Some of these examples are designed to suggest books or other texts that may make useful sources for comparison (or for complementary purposes) when you are reading Atwood's work. Again, they may be related to literary or critical themes, or they may be relevant to social and cultural themes current 'then' or 'now'.

Focus on: the theme of utopias and dystopias

— *The Handmaid's Tale* is a 'dystopia' – that is, a story about an imaginary world and state of society where things have gone wrong. The 'dys' part comes from the Greek and means a malfunction (as in 'muscular dystrophy', for instance). But the whole word 'dystopia' is based on the word 'utopia', which derives from a fiction written in 1516 by Thomas More called *Utopia*. This was a portrait of an ideal state, and again his invented name for his island state of Utopia was derived from the Greek. Look up both words in a dictionary. See Dominic Baker-Smith's *More's Utopia* (1991), in the Unwin Critical Library series, for an excellent introduction to Thomas More and his book.

Since Thomas More's work there have been many other 'utopian' fictions, which very often include some 'dystopian' features. An ideal world for one set of people may not be ideal for another group of people. Some of the best-known of these fictions include Aldous Huxley's *Brave New World* (1932), George Orwell's *Nineteen Eighty-Four* (1949), William Morris's *The News from Nowhere* (1891), Samuel Butler's *Erewhon* (1872) and Yevgeny Zamyatin's *We* (1920). You might like to look at one of two of these and compare the societies portrayed there with the regime of Gilead in *The Handmaid's Tale*.

In Anne Cranny-Francis, *Feminist Fiction: Feminist Uses of Generic Fiction* (1990), pp. 107–42 you will find a chapter on 'Feminist Utopias'. It gives a summary of the history of utopian fiction, before coming on to the many feminist utopian fictions of the late twentieth century, and on to the dystopian *The Handmaid's Tale*.

Some other utopias (and dystopias) are to be found in Charlotte Perkins Gilman's *Herland* (1916), Ursula Le Guin's *The Dispossessed: An Ambiguous Utopia* (1974), Dorothy Byant's *The*

Kin of Ata Are Waiting for You (first published as *The Comforter* in 1971), Joanna Russ's *The Female Man* (1975), Mary Staton's *From the Legend of Biel* (1975), James Tiptree Junior's '*Houston, Houston, do you read?*' (1976), Marge Piercy's *Woman on the Edge of Time* (1976), Suzy McKee Charnas's *Motherlines* (1978) and Sally Miller Gearhart's *The Wanderground* (1978).

COMPARE . . .

— Read Act II, scene 1 of Shakespeare's *The Tempest* where Gonzalo begins a speech with 'If I had plantation of this island . . . and were the king on 't.' In what ways can Gonzalo's ideas be compared with the ideas behind the regime in Gilead?

— Read Part III, Chapter 3 of Angela Carter's *Nights at the Circus* (1984) where you will find a description of a fantasy women's prison hidden in the steppes of Russia. The rules and the rebellions in the prison are described there. How might the regimen compare with what is prescribed by the laws of Gilead? And how might the ways in which the women prisoners resist their persecutors be compared with the ways in which Offred, Ofglen and Moira behave in *The Handmaid's Tale*?

Focus on: social satire

RESEARCH . . .

— Look up satire and social satire in the glossary of literary terms. Two works by Jonathan Swift – *Gulliver's Travels* (1726) and *A Modest Proposal* (1729) – are social satires, criticising in an amusing and inventive way certain practices and assumptions current in the eighteenth century. Another well-known social satire is George Orwell's *Animal Farm* (1945), in which the rule of the pigs over other farmyard animals criticised (through fable) the rise of totalitarian regimes, both on the left and the right, in the early twentieth century. Compare Atwood's use of satire with Swift's or Orwell's.

Focus on: extraordinary (and not so extraordinary) social and political conditions

COMPARE AND CONTRAST . . .

Atwood has said that there is nothing in *The Handmaid's Tale* that hasn't already happened or isn't happening elsewhere. The restrictive circumstances under which women (and men) live in the state of Gilead are based on many historical circumstances, and on present political situations. In the interview she refers to the rise of far-right fundamentalist politics in the United States, as well as to the practices of late twentieth-century regimes in Iran and Afghanistan.

— Research some of these historical situations. In Afghanistan, for instance, the religious rulers known as the Taliban, interpreting the strictures of Islam, introduced a variety of laws that are similar to those prevalent in Gilead. In 2001 they destroyed two famous and ancient Buddhas in the region of Bamian, on the grounds that they were 'shrines of infidels'. In another decree all writing on paper bags was banned, in case it should quote holy words and these would be defiled by being treated with disrespect, as rubbish. Many acts that might be considered disobedient or resistant, rather than strictly criminal, were punished with severity. Amputations and executions, for instance, would be carried out in public in football stadiums, witnessed by huge crowds.

— Find out as much as you can about similar practices, both in the past and in the present, and compare them to the methods of rule in Gilead.

CONSIDER THE POSITION OF WOMEN . . .

— It is of course the position of women that takes up the main strand of argument in *The Handmaid's Tale*. Look at this list of respective duties, taken from a 1614 text on marriage by John Dod and Robert Cleaver, called 'A Godly Forme of Householde Gouernment':

Husband	*Wife*
Deal with many men	Talk with few
Be 'entertaining'	Be solitary and withdrawn
Be skilful in talk	Boast of silence

— How might these rules of deportment compare with what you find in *The Handmaid's Tale*?
— More recently, under the extremist religious regime in Afghanistan in the early twenty-first century, women were forbidden to work and were required to rely on their male relatives for support. To learn more about these circumstances you might read Saira Shah's book *The Story-Teller's Daughter* (2003), which tells about her various visits to Afghanistan, both while it was occupied by Russia in the late twentieth century and while it was ruled by the Taliban. Saira Shah also made two television documentaries for Channel 4, called *Beneath the Veil* and *Unholy War*.

In some countries forced marriages are common. One such story is told in Zana Muhsen's book *Sold: One Woman's True Account of Modern Slavery*. In 1980 she and her sister Nadia, aged fifteen and fourteen, were taken by their father from their home in Birmingham to be married in their native country of the Yemen. Muhsen followed that up with another book, *A Promise to Nadia: The True Story of a British Slave* (2001).

Conventions restricting women are not only to be found outside the West, nor are they always imposed from outside by official orders. In Britain, women soldiers are at present

(2002) still not permitted to join front-line units such as the SAS (Special Air Service), in spite of the fact that the Human Rights Act and the European Union's Charter of Human Rights suggest that these roles should be available to women, just as they are to men. The official grounds for the British Government's decision are that less than 2 per cent of servicewomen are as fit as servicemen, and that women soldiers are eight times more prone to injury than men.

As for movements and trends that voluntarily legislate for women, you might like to look at a book that was a bestseller in the United States, written by Laura Doyle and called *The Surrendered Wife: A practical guide to finding intimacy, passion and peace with a man* (2001).

FIND OUT ABOUT SUMPTUARY LAWS . . .

— The sumptuary laws – regulating what you may and may not wear – portrayed in *The Handmaid's Tale* have sources both in the past and in the present. Look up 'sumptuary laws' in a dictionary. During the Middle Ages, and later, these often related to matters of class and rank, but also to the status of women. See Chapter 5 of Lisa Jardine's book *Still Harping on Daughters: Women and Drama in the Age of Shakespeare* (1983), where you will find tables and accounts of sixteenth-century dress codes, sumptuary laws and the 'natural order'.

As for the present day, Ann Treneman wrote an article called 'The Invisible Woman' in *The Times* (13 November 2001), pp. 2–4, about her experiences as she went about London for one day wearing a burka. But, as with Offred and Moira, certain kinds of resistance to rules and expectations are made by the women governed by such requirements, whether secular or religious. The photography of the Iranian artist Shadi Ghadirian is one example, where she portrays her contemporaries in conventional dress but subverts the image with the inclusion of 'forbidden' objects, such as Pepsi cans, ghetto blasters and bicycles.

CONSIDER QUESTIONS TO DO WITH INFERTILITY . . .

— One of the underlying problems that has resulted in the establishment of the restrictive laws about procreation that are portrayed in *The Handmaid's Tale* is the fact that this imaginary country has suffered a drastic reduction in its birth rate. This is explained in the 'Historical Notes' that look back on the text. In some ways this is still a contemporary issue in the West. Find out about these concerns; about medical interventions such as IVF (in vitro fertilisation); about surrogate motherhood. As Atwood explains in the interview, the idea of surrogate motherhood is not new – she refers to the story of Rachel and Leah from the Bible, Genesis, Chapter 30. Research such practices in history and in the past, and consider how they relate to the themes of *The Handmaid's Tale*.

Focus on: men and women

SWAP AND COMPARE JOKES . . .

On pp. 233–4 there is a joke. '"Is anything wrong, dear?" the old joke went. "No, why!" "You moved".' It's a joke about sex and about men's and women's attitudes to sex. Underlying the joke is a range of assumptions about man's superior position. Sexist jokes of all kinds promote and preserve these assumptions. Here are two examples:

- How do you keep a woman in the kitchen? Shorten her chain.
- Why are women's feet so small? So they can get nearer the sink.

— Ask around your friends and make a list of jokes along these lines. Then sit down and think about why they are funny, if they are funny, or why they aren't funny.

— Then consider how what might seem the most banal behaviour could become a platform for more serious political consequences for women – and for men – as it does in *The Handmaid's Tale*.

— Ask yourself what other groups jokes discriminate against: for instance, foreigners, ethnic groups, disabled people, gays. When you think about such jokes, remember that they all include an element to do with power. They might also include an element of fear.

Words, language, writing and reading

RESEARCH AND CONSIDER . . .

— There is a great deal in *The Handmaid's Tale* about words and language, and about how language can be manipulated and abused, exploited and revised, for political purposes. Offred – as one who is composing a subversive narrative, as one who is forbidden to read – thinks a great deal about this manipulation of words. One of the ways in which the state of Gilead exerts power over its people is by decreeing how language will be used, by inventing terms that are derogatory or hierarchical. In other words they create a language that is politically motivated if not 'politically correct'. Think about the ways that language can be made 'politically correct' today. You might like to read Deborah Cameron's book *Verbal Hygiene* (1995), which includes a chapter called 'Civility and its discontents: Language and political correctness', pp. 116–65. It also includes a chapter on women and language entitled 'The new Pygmalion: verbal hygiene for women', pp. 166–211, where she discusses many issues that could relate to the depiction of the coercion of women in *The Handmaid's Tale*.

Narrative and storytelling

COMPARE AND CONSIDER . . .
— We never know where Offred's narrative is coming from, to whom she imagines she is speaking, or whether or not she can be trusted – though some (suspect) pieces of information are given to us in the 'Historical Notes'. If you look at the interview you will see that Atwood is intrigued by methods of storytelling. You might like to compare the modes used in some of her other books with that used in *The Handmaid's Tale*. Good titles to choose might be *Lady Oracle* (1976) or *Cat's Eye* (1989).

VINTAGE
LIVING
TEXTS

Bluebeard's Egg

IN CLOSE-UP

Reading guides for

BLUEBEARD'S EGG

BEFORE YOU BEGIN TO READ . . .

— Look at the interview with Atwood. You will see there that she mentions a number of themes in this book, including:

- Men and women
- Mothers
- The question of first, second or third person
- Audience
- Time
- Narrative methods

Other themes that you might also consider include:

- Oral histories
- 'Canadian literature'
- The Gothic
- The idea of the Muse
- Food
- The colour blue
- Fairy stories

SHORT STORY COLLECTION OR NOVEL? . . .

— Think about the wording on the front cover of the novel and the differences between this and the title pages. The front cover and half title page state simply 'Bluebeard's Egg', but on the title page the wording is slightly different: 'Bluebeard's Egg and Other Stories'.

— Explore the differences between these two titles. In what ways are your expectations for a collection of short stories different from those for a novel? What kinds of demands do short stories make on the reader? How does having a contents page alter your initial ideas about the text?

— When you have finished the text, re-examine these questions. Discuss, or explore individually, how your ideas about collections of short stories have changed. Do you now think about them differently in relation to novels?

Focus on: the title

RESEARCH . . .

— Atwood's collection refers to a specific myth – the myth of Bluebeard. This was most famously recorded by Charles Perrault in his 1697 collection of fairy stories, but who is Bluebeard? What is his story? (Think about this as you read the stories about the echo of this myth throughout the book. Where do you come across parallel stories, or references specifically to the myth?)

— Read the section about the metaphorical significance of the colour blue in Marina Warner's *From the Beast to the Blonde: Fairy Tales and Their Tellers* (1996). What other associations with the colour blue can you make? For instance, what does it mean to feel 'blue'? What are 'the blues'? What is a 'blue' steak? In Australia a red-headed man is often called 'Bluey' – can you guess why? When you've come up with a list of references and allusions, look through the collection of stories and see how many 'blue' references there are, then consider how they might complicate your overall reading of the title.

Reading activities: detailed analysis

SIGNIFICANT MOMENTS IN THE LIFE OF MY MOTHER
SECTION I (pp. 11–17)

Focus on: the theme of childhood

CONSIDER . . .

— This short story opens with 'significant' moments of childhood from both the narrator herself and her mother. Think about the selective narratives given in this opening section.

— Consider the treatment of 'growing up' in this section: list the different types of pain experienced (for example, physical, psychological, emotional) and who experiences them. Explore for whom these types of pain are 'growing pains' linked to the transition from childhood to adulthood.

COMPARE AND EVALUATE . . .

— Contrast the two treatments of 'haircuts' (pp. 14–15) – how do they mark a 'significant' threshold? Compare the details of the stories, and find similarities and differences. How does the narrator establish the theme of childhood and adolescence in this opening section? (Think about the phrase 'hair-raising'.)

DISCUSS . . .

— What story do you remember and consider 'significant' in marking the boundary for you between childhood and adolescence? Think about how that story parallels the ones in this section. How is your story 'significant' in relation to those in the book?

SECTION 2 (pp. 17–23)

Focus on: language and style

EXAMINE AND ASSESS . . .

— This section features the narrator's mother on a long car journey where she is unable to tell her fellow passengers that the cat on her knee has had an accident (pp. 19–20). There is a discussion of what different groups of people 'can' and 'cannot' say. The text sets up distinct groups: for example, younger/older, and men/women. Consider the following:

- How does the language of this section highlight a gap between what you say and what you mean?
- How do different groups come to understand different meanings from the same words?
- 'In those days, things like that . . . were not mentioned' (p. 19). Examine the different metaphors that the narrator uses to establish these different groups, concentrating on the division between *either* the generations *or* the sexes.

SECTION 3 (pp. 24–9)

Focus on: genre

RESEARCH AND EXPLORE . . .

— Think about the style of this final section. 'There is, however, a difference between symbolism and anecdote,' we are told (p. 27). The story mimics certain literary genres: autobiography and biography. Discover what these two genres are and discuss the differences between them.

— Examine the language in this section. How does it support the expectations of a 'biography' or 'autobiography'? For example, count the number of times 'my mother' or 'my father' is used and consider the impact of the repetition on you as a reader.

— Come back to this discussion at the end of the collection and think about the relationship of these genres to the stories as a whole.

HURRICANE HAZEL
SECTION 1 (pp. 31–4)

Focus on: tone and language

LIST AND DESCRIBE . . .

— Look at the language that is used to describe the narrator's house. List the adjectives employed to give the reader a sense of her surroundings. Look at the particular language used: for example, references to 'parachutes' (pp. 31, 32) and 'war surplus' (p. 32). Evaluate why there is so much detail, and what it evokes. How is the tone of the story is set through this detailed description?

SECTION 2 (pp. 34–52)

Focus on: the theme of forms of writing

IDENTIFY AND ASSESS . . .

— 'Many words were enclosed by quotation marks' (pp. 36–7).

This story features various types of writing: love letters from Buddy, as well as attempted replies; letters from the narrator's brother, textbooks and novels. Choose one form of writing and consider how it contributes to the theme of communication in the collection. For example, you might look at the idea of translation by looking at the Greek textbook (p. 42), or the idea of honest writing and 'forgery' (pp. 43–4) in the love letters. You might examine the idea of technical forms of writing – 'Even I knew what a zygote was' (p. 49) – and how 'educational' forms of writing suggest a hierarchy within the story. How does this alienate Buddy from his girl?

— Think about how one specific type of writing contrasts with the voice of the narrator *telling* you about the forms of writing.

Focus on: the theme of romance

CONSIDER . . .

— 'Buddy was a lot older than I was. He was eighteen . . . He had his own car . . . he smoked and drank beer' (p. 37). This section (pp. 37–41) features the dates that Buddy and the narrator have. Look at the portrayal of Buddy, and examine closely the descriptions both of him and of the events of the evening: how does Atwood play upon ideas about 'romance', 'dating' and attraction – is the account romantic, humorous?

SECTION 3 (pp. 52–9)

Focus on: literary reference

RESEARCH AND ASSESS . . .

— On p. 52 there is a reference to *The Mill on the Floss* (1860) by George Eliot. That novel's thematic concerns parallel the concerns of this story. If you can, read *The Mill on the Floss* and compare the novel's focus on ideas of romance, and becoming a woman, as well as the relationship of natural disasters to emotional upheaval, with the story's focus. When you have thought about the themes that occur strongly in both texts, think about the ways in which these themes are also the focus of other stories in the collection.

— Look for other literary allusions in the story as a whole. For example, who wrote *Wuthering Heights* (1847), and what is the novel about? How do these references to other novels in this story inform the collection as a whole?

Focus on: the theme of weather

DISCOVER . . .

— Find the meaning of the phrase 'pathetic fallacy'. How does Atwood use the 'pathetic fallacy' in this scene?

EXPLORE . . .

— Think about how this literary construct operates in the novels that the book refers to – both *Wuthering Heights* and *The Mill on the Floss* feature famous interventions of the weather.

LOULOU: OR, THE DOMESTIC LIFE OF THE LANGUAGE
SECTION I (pp. 61–70)

Focus on: the theme of 'arts' versus 'crafts'

ANALYSE . . .

— Look at the opening paragraphs and the description of Loulou, who sets herself physically apart from her apprentices: 'She doesn't consider them suitable for wedging clay, with their puny little biceps' (p. 61). Search this section for references to

'clay', and analyse the portrayal of Loulou as a 'potter' (p. 61). What does this section suggest that it means to be a 'potter'?
— The story sets up a distinction between the potter and 'the poets' (p. 61). Look particularly at the last paragraph on pp. 64–5 and detail the distinctions drawn between an *artist* and a *craftsman*. What differences does this paragraph draw attention to and how does this theme feature in the rest of the section? Think about the means by which Loulou represents the 'crafts' while the poets are 'artists'.
— When you have worked on this section, look at the accountant's version of Loulou (pp. 74–5). How does this complicate the idea of the 'artist' as evidenced in the attitudes of both Loulou and the poets?

Focus on: the theme of naming

DETAIL AND DISCUSS . . .
Atwood establishes the name 'Loulou' as having certain 'connotations' – if you aren't sure what this means, investigate the term. We are told that people frequently pay a great deal of attention to Loulou's name (pp. 65–7).
— Throughout this section the poets attempt to name Loulou in other ways – at the outset she is called 'marmoreal' (p. 61). Pick out examples of the ways in which the poets attempt to 'name' Loulou. Discover what they mean, if you are unsure, and discuss the extent to which the various 'names' that the poets give Loulou influence your perception of her.
— Equally, look at Loulou's reaction to this process of 'naming'. How does she negotiate with the poets? To what extent is she under their authority as they name her and she becomes an object to be named? Does her reaction undermine this naming process?
— When you have discussed Loulou's reaction to the attempt to 'name' her, think about the theme of naming in the stories

79

you have read so far. How many other narrators' or protagonists' names are you given? Is Loulou the narrator of this story? How does that change your attitude?

SECTION 2 (pp. 70–81)

Focus on: the theme of seduction

CONSIDER . . .

— 'It's another day, and Loulou is on her way to seduce her accountant' (p. 70). The narrative at this point traces Loulou's seduction of the accountant (pp. 70–9). Is Loulou constructed as the seducer, as opposed to the 'victim'? How does this incident invert stereotyped sexual roles, or does it reaffirm them?

— Look at the dialogue of the incident and consider how the language of seduction is played with in this section. Does Loulou seduce the accountant verbally? If not, examine the means by which her aim is achieved. Through analysing the language, come to a decision about the extent to which you consider Loulou to be the subject or object of seduction.

Focus on: jokes and humour

EVALUATE . . .

— In this same section (pp. 70–81) think about Atwood's employment of humour. One of the poets comments that 'Loulou is to *subdued* as Las Vegas at night is to a sixty-watt light bulb' (p. 71). Look at the descriptions of the seduction and its context (that is, where the seduction takes place). How does humour inform and undermine the rhetoric of seduction here? Evaluate the extent to which this is indeed a seduction narrative, and the ways in which this is undermined by the humour of the story.

DISCUSS . . .

— Would you want to characterise this narrative as a 'comedy' rather than a 'seduction'? Having evaluated the different styles operating within the story, discuss what genre of story you would consider it to be in the light of your close reading. Has your view changed, and if so, how?

UGLYPUSS
SECTION I (pp. 83–93)

Focus on: the theme of belonging

EXAMINE AND COMPARE . . .

— Joel and Becka are both preoccupied with whether or not they are a part of particular communities. Becka regards Joel's 'La-Z-Boy' chair as being 'the essence' of 'bourgeoisie'. What does it mean to be a member of the bourgeoisie? Do the couple fight to belong to the 'bourgeois' class, or are they establishing that they are excluded from it?

— Joel, equally, is attacked for his treatment of 'Jewish' issues as an artist. What does Joel do to force his exclusion from this community? How does the rejection of the community affect Joel's sense of identity?

Focus on: vocabulary

RESEARCH AND ANALYSE . . .

— In this story Atwood cites a great deal of Jewish or Yiddish vocabulary. Pick out the particular terms used – there are events such as 'Yom Kippur', as well as words like 'shul' (p. 85) and 'shtick' (p. 87), 'shmuck' and 'goy'. Find out what the Jewish vocabulary in this section means. Then think about what effect the use of a specific vocabulary has on the narrative. How does this vocabulary highlight the thematic concern with belonging mentioned above?

— Alternatively, scan the text for a 'corporate' vocabulary. How does the use of sentences like 'He types out a note – writing would be too intimate – saying he's been called out suddenly, to an important meeting, and he'll talk to her later' (pp. 90–1) suggest a particular set of business or 'power' relationships within this section?

— How is the use of the vocabulary of business and class tied to Joel's reference to the 'bourgeoisie' as highlighted above? How is a 'corporate' vocabulary used to ironise the breakdown of Joel's and Becka's relationship?

SECTION 2 (pp. 93–103)

Focus on: the theme of gender

LIST AND EXPLORE . . .

At the opening of this section Becka returns from the toilets and repeats a quotation she's just read: 'Women make love. Men make war' (p. 93). This part of the story is particularly interested in gender stereotyping and gender roles. Later in the section (p. 96) Joel grapples with the different kinds of versions of womanhood that he encounters and finds attractive.

— Work your way through the section, picking up on excerpts like the ones suggested above and exploring the gender divisions as drawn in this story. Examine the references to the politicisation of gender, as when Joel thinks, 'He's never seen the point of rape' (p. 96) or when he uses the phrase 'patriarchal paternalism' (p. 100). Discover what these phrases mean and then think about the ways in which this section makes an argument about gender.

— How does Atwood suggest that Joel regards some of his behaviour as 'male'? What does it mean, in this story to behave like a 'man'? How does the story critique the consequences of these versions of gender for women, through Becka and Amelia?

Focus on: the theme of history and conflict

COMPARE AND DISCUSS . . .
— 'We're talking about *history*' (p. 94). Think about the relationship of history (as a version of events) to conflict in this text. Compare Amelia's choice of reading in the restaurant to Becka's fight about a female version of history. When Joel discovers his flat has been trashed, he refers to Becka as a 'histrionic bitch' (p. 102). Compare the different references to history in this section and how they are used to complicate one another.
— When you have considered this, you might want to discuss its relationship to the Jewish community, which is the focus of the first section of the narrative, and think about that historic conflict and oppression in relation to the theme of conflict as it is traced in personal relationships.

SECTION 3 (pp. 103–10)

Focus on: narrative voices

EXAMINE . . .
— On p. 103, after a short gap, the narrative shifts from Joel to Becka. How does this change in narrative voice alter our attitude towards the story itself? How does the narrator gain our sympathy by speaking to us in the first person? How does it alter your perception of Becka as depicted by Joel? Look at Becka's version of 'uglypuss' as opposed to Joel's. How does this establish the difference that perspective makes in the reader's attitude to the stories we are being told?

Focus on: the theme of love

INTERPRET . . .

— Becka's narrative considers at length the question of love. How does she use the cat, 'Uglypuss', as a complex metaphor for love (pp. 106–7)? Think about the other kinds of love that Becka refers to in this section, such as familial love and religious love.

— The story finishes with her asserting that '*My heart does not bleed*, she tells herself, but it does' (p. 110). Expand upon the relationship between love and suffering suggested here. Where else does Becka talk about the demands of love and the kinds of suffering she undergoes, both while in love and when being rejected by a loved one?

DISCOVER AND RE-INTERPRET . . .

— The reference in 'my heart does not bleed' (p. 110) is a religious allusion to the 'Sacred Heart'. Find out what the Sacred Heart' is. How does it inform Becka's version of love and suffering in the text?

TWO STORIES ABOUT EMMA

Focus on: subdivisions, sections and parts

CONCEPTUALISE . . .

— Before working on the two stories, think about the decision to have two stories closely tied under one title. How does this change your expectations for these two sections and the links between them?

— How does the theme of water in the titles give you a clue as to the conceptual links between the two 'stories about Emma'?

— Reconceptualise this relationship after you have looked at the two stories, and then again when you have read the collection as a whole.

THE WHIRLPOOL RAPIDS
SECTION I (pp. 111–19)

Focus on: the theme of miracles

ANALYSE . . .
— pp. 111 and 112 form the opening section to the stories in that they are demarcated from the rest of the text. How does the opening set up thematic concerns about Emma's exceptional nature? How are religious themes established in her invulnerability to physical danger? Give this particular consideration when you read the second of the 'two stories about Emma': 'Walking on Water'. How are parallels established between Emma and Christ in this opening section?

Focus on: the theme of chance or risk

EVALUATE . . .
— 'It was a freak accident, and the fact that she was there at all was an accident too, the result of a whim' (pp. 112). Select the points in the narrative where the narrator reiterates the 'freak' nature of Emma's presence at Niagara and on the ride itself. How does Atwood examine the idea of 'fate' in this story? What narrative strategies does the text use to remind the reader of the role of 'chance' in Emma's story?

RESEARCH AND DISCUSS . . .
— Why does Atwood choose to set the tale at Niagara Falls (the text gives some clues as to the area's history) (p. 114)? Find

out about the risks taken at the falls and discuss how a knowledge of the context complicates the narrative version of Emma's risk. Does an understanding of the falls' reputation for danger alter your perception of the narrator's discussion of the 'freak' nature of Emma's accident?

Focus on: the theme of 'telling' and 'listening'

EXAMINE AND ANALYSE . . .

— 'Emma has told me that she learned several things from this experience' (p. 118). Examine the ways in which the moral to this story is constructed. Pick out the number of times Emma is implicated directly: 'the most obvious effect of the accident on Emma' (p. 119), or indirectly: 'She never thought to herself' (p. 118). What is the effect upon 'the listener' that the storyteller and the narrator are not the same person? How does Atwood's use of the anonymous third-person narrator make the story less didactic? How does Atwood construct the 'moral' of the story?

LIST . . .

— What sort of story does this remind you of? What kinds of stories give you a sense of the point of them, at the end?
— Create a working list of the kinds of 'telling' at work in this story. For example, is it a biography or a parable? (Be careful to be clear about how the kinds of stories differ from one another.)

LINK . . .

— Using the list you have just constructed, think about how these genres link with the other stories in the collection, both those preceding and those following 'Two Stories about Emma'. Keep this list as a working one, annotating it as you consider different stories. Which genres occur again and again, and how are they manipulated in different ways in the stories you identify?

WALKING ON WATER
SECTION 1 (pp. 120–9)

Focus on: the theme of water

EVALUATE . . .
— Select the various different types of water you find in both 'Walking on Water', and 'The Whirlpool Rapids'. Think about what differentiates these types of water, then explore these differences. So, for example, when thinking about the River 'Nile' (p. 120), evaluate both how this is characterised in terms of 'rivers' as opposed to 'rapids', and what particular resonances the 'Nile' has in contrast to the discussion of 'Niagara Falls' in Emma's first story.

RESEARCH . . .
— If you don't know anything about the Nile, do some research to help your understanding of the location.

CHARACTERISE . . .
— When you have formed an understanding of the different types of water, think about how it is employed thematically to characterise different facets of the story. For example, how does the title 'Walking on Water' set up a very particular relationship to the varying forms of water in the stories? Characterise this relationship in terms of how it alters your perception of the various incidents involving water in the preceding story.

Focus on: the theme of miracles

DISCOVER AND INTERPRET . . .
Throughout this section there are references to trickery. The idea of the exceptional permeates both stories, and the title highlights a particularly famous Christian 'miracle': Jesus walking on water.

87

— Find out which Christian incident in particular is being referred to. Either ask someone or use resources like the Internet to do an accelerated Bible search. When you have discovered the particular narrative that Atwood is invoking, consider how it influences your reading of the story.

— What is the link between 'miracles' and 'trickery'? How is 'illusion' treated in the story? How does the narrative play with the idea of 'miracles'? To what extent does Atwood construct 'Emma' as a 'Christ' figure?

RECONSIDER . . .

— When you have thought about the relationship of 'Emma' to 'Christ' through 'miracles', go back and think about the biblical narrative construction used in the first story. Compare the endings of the two tales. To what extent do they both read like parables? How does Christian mythology link the two stories to one another? Is it undermined through the association of parables and miracles with illusion and trickery?

BLUEBEARD'S EGG
SECTION I (pp. 131–41)

Focus on: the title

RELATE . . .

— Think about the centrality of this story to the collection, and how it is central both physically and in terms of the title. How does this privilege the story in terms of the collection? Think about whether or not the thematic concerns of the story reflect the main concerns of the collection. Were you tempted to read this story first? If so, did you?

— When you have finished the collection, reconsider the issue of this story's centrality.

RESEARCH . . .
— If you didn't discover what the Bluebeard myth is when considering the beginning of the collection, discover what the myth is now. How does this story deviate from the original Bluebeard myth? Myths are about teaching social behaviour, so think about the relationship of myth in this story to the use Margaret Atwood makes of parables in the previous stories.

Focus on: the number three

LIST AND ANALYSE . . .
— Consider the significance of the number three in this opening section. This is one way in which this story resembles the genre of the fairy tale.
— Identify other examples of this genre at work in the narrative – for example, how do we read phrases like 'the inevitable happens' (p. 136) or the idea of preparing for a journey (pp. 140–1) in comparison to fairy tales like *Hansel and Gretel*? How does fairy-tale logic affect your reading of the story as a whole – how does it alter your expectations?
— Analyse how 'fairy-tale' logic sets up specific preconceptions in the reader. How does Atwood manipulate this understanding? For example, how is it used in this first section to set up certain expectations for the story? How does putting Sally in the role of the third wife alter our expectations of her, as a result of this logic?

Focus on: narrative structure and 'subversion'

DETAIL AND EXPLORE . . .
— 'Sally is in love with Ed because of his stupidity, his monumental and almost energetic stupidity' (p. 132). 'Ed isn't threatened . . . He's so dumb it doesn't occur to him she might not be joking'(p. 140). Examine the textual references to Ed's 'stupidity' in this opening section. How does Atwood set up Ed's

89

'stupidity' so that we are suspicious of it, even when it is being stated? How does Sally's version of his idiocy undermine, or subvert, itself?

— Explore the means by which the overt statement has 'subverted' Sally's narrative so that by the second section we are ready to disbelieve it.

SECTION 2 (pp. 141–9)

Focus on: the theme of cookery and food

CONSIDER . . .

— Look at the opening paragraph of this section. Consider Atwood's use of the theme of cookery and preparation (pp. 141–3, 147). Look both backward and forward, at the opening of the story (p. 131) and at the final section (pp. 160–4). How is the preparation and consumption of food used as a narrative framework for the story? How does Atwood employ it to link the various parts of the story together?

CHARACTERISE . . .

— When you have thought about the theme of food and cookery and how it binds the parts of the stories together, consider how different characters' attitudes to food differentiates them. For example, paying particular attention to Ed, how is his relationship to food used as a mode of characterisation? Think about this in relation to the discussion of the 'subversion' of Ed's stupidity. How is this evidenced in the theme of food and cookery?

Focus on: the theme of 'games'

EXAMINE . . .

— 'When the kids were younger, Sally used to play Monopoly

90

with them' (p. 148). Why does Atwood give such a detailed version of the 'game' of Monopoly?

— Think about how different people's attitudes to the game are established. How does this version of Ed complicate Sally's discussion of his 'stupidity' in Section 1?

ASK YOURSELF . . .

— Consider the other types of 'games' played in the narrative, both literal and allegorical. Pay particular attention to Ed's relationship with both Sally and Marylynn, and think about who is playing games with whom?

SECTION 3 (pp. 150–64)

Focus on: oral narratives and fairy tale

INTERPRET AND DISCUSS . . .

— '"Explore your inner world," said Sally's instructor in *Forms of Narrative Fiction*' (p. 150). This section of the novel considers closely the relationship of oral to textual narratives. Look at Sally's discussion of this (pp. 153–4). What are the problems she delineates?

— What oral narratives do you identify for your community? Are they 'urban myths'? Or 'fairy tales'? Discuss in a group the narratives that this section conjures up for you. How are they complicated when they are written down?

LIST AND EVALUATE . . .

— Look at the retelling of the Bluebeard narrative (pp. 154–7). How many narrators of this 'myth' are there?

— Sally is asked to re*write* the story from a different 'point of view'. Think about the relationship here of 'writing' to 'telling'.

— What is the consequence for the story when you consider how many voices it is being translated through?

— Think about changing stories, and the difference between telling and writing them differently. Link this back to your consideration of 'games'.

PLAY AND DISCUSS . . .

— In order to remind yourself about the complexities of oral narratives, play a game of 'Chinese whispers'. Afterwards discuss the idea of narrative ownership. Does the story belong to the first teller, the last, or the person who made the 'change' when the meaning altered.

— Now go back to the story as a whole and think about the relationship of meaning to ownership. To what extent does Sally attempt to 'own' the narrative by writing it, as opposed to telling it?

Focus on: the theme of the Egg

CONSIDER . . .

— 'This is something the story left out, Sally thinks: the egg is alive, and one day it will hatch. But what will come out of it?' (p. 164). Look at Sally's version of the 'Egg'. What do you perceive it to represent for her?

EXPAND . . .

— Think about the significance of the egg both for this story and for the collection as a whole: to what extent is the 'Egg' the conceptual centre of the novel?

SPRING SONG OF THE FROGS
SECTION I (pp. 165–72)

Focus on: the theme of nature

EXAMINE . . .

— Look particularly carefully at the language of the opening section (pp. 165–72), paying attention to phrases like 'wax and wane' (p. 165) and the use of colour: 'mulberry' (p. 165), 'golden' (p. 169) and 'peach' (p. 172). Examine the way 'natural' language is employed in this section. How are the seasons used to conjure up ideas about natural development? How is the moon employed? (When you have looked at the treatment of the moon in this section, take your examination through to the end of the story: who is Diane? How does the moon frame the story?)

EVALUATE . . .

— Compare the use of this 'natural' descriptive language to the women Will is describing. How are metaphors of the seasons and weather, as well as the natural landscape, used to suggest what is 'natural' about the women? When considering these questions, pay particular attention to the section devoted to Will's visit to Cynthia in hospital (pp. 168–72).

DISCUSS . . .

— When you have pinpointed the way in which this section plays upon ideas about 'natural' behaviour, discuss this theme in relation to the collection as a whole. For example, how does the treatment of 'natural' in this story relate to the text's consideration of 'normal' in the opening tale, 'Significant Moments in the Life of My Mother'?

SECTION 2 (pp. 172–8)

Focus on: the theme of memory

COMPARE AND EVALUATE . . .

'"I wanted you to hear the frogs" . . . This doesn't have the effect on Will he has hoped it would. The voices coming from the darkness below the curve of the hill sound thin and ill. There aren't as many frogs as there used to be, either.' (p. 178).
— In this story we encounter Will's relationship with three women. Paying particular attention to this final section, look at how the theme of memory mediates Will's narration. How does the reader come to know Diane through his version of her as he remembers her?
— Pick out particular phrases that demonstrate how our knowledge of Diane is constructed in terms of Will's memories of her. Then go back to 'Bluebeard's Egg' and compare the final sections of the two stories. Think about the similarities and differences between Will's version of Diane and Sally's version of Marylynn. Concentrate on the difference in tenses and on how hearing about an event in the present tense alters our understanding of it as opposed to Will's narration of memory.

SCARLET IBIS
SECTION I (pp. 179–85)

Focus on: language and tone

CHARACTERISE . . .

— '"You felt tired before," Christine said. "That's why we came, remember?"' (p. 179). The opening section of this story creates a powerful atmosphere of strain. Consider *how* Atwood evokes such a feeling.

— Look at her characterisation of the main characters' behaviour: how is Lilian's restlessness suggested?

— Look at Christine's version of the opening of their 'holiday'. How is the idea of the 'holiday' manipulated to add to the feeling of frustration and tension?

SECTION 2 (pp. 185–99)

Focus on: the themes of pilgrimage and religion

RESEARCH . . .

— Discover what a 'Mennonite' and a 'Scarlet Ibis' are: either ask someone or use reference materials.

CONSIDER AND DISCUSS . . .

— Once you have established the meaning of these terms, think about the consequence of Atwood's choices for the story – pick out one or two of the questions below that particularly interest you and, having developed your responses, discuss them as a group.

- How does her employment of a particular religious discourse alter the story?
- What is a 'pilgrimage'? Think about how Christine, Don and Lilian's journey can be understood to be a pilgrimage.
- To what extent does the 'Ibis' save the family?
- Think about the idea of 'sacrifice'. How is this tied to the theme of religion in the story? Pay particular attention to the relationship of Christine and the Mennonite woman (pp. 188, 195): how are their sacrifices an essential part of the journey?

THE SALT GARDEN
SECTION I (pp. 201–8)

Focus on: the theme of experimentation

LIST, DISTINGUISH AND ANALYSE . . .

— Taking the title as your starting point, list the varying types of experimentation delineated in this section. Perhaps separate each of the characters out and look at their particular experimentations – for example, the different things Carol has experimented with (pp. 201–4), as opposed to Alma's references to 'Acid flashes' (p. 205).

— Once you have a list, distinguish and analyse the differences between various kinds of experimentation. For instance, the idea of scientific experimentation is treated very differently socially from that of sexual or emotional experimentation. Also consider the ways in which Atwood plays with these differences. How does she juxtapose them, for example, and how is Alma's consideration of her daughter's experimentation complicated by her attitude to Mort's?

SECTION 2 (pp. 208–19)

Focus on: the theme of apocalypse

SELECT AND DISCUSS . . .

— The previous section has established Alma's collapse. At the opening of this section she interprets these 'fits' very differently from her partner's. She suggests that it is not a personal but a cultural phenomenon (pp. 208–9). Look closely at her version of medieval panic and compare Alma's version of this historical trauma with her own hallucinations. What signs does she pinpoint as reinforcing her notion of 'the end of the world' (p. 211)?

— 'Sometimes she tells herself this isn't the first time people have thought they were coming to the end of the world . . . which Alma remembers as having been one of the high points of second-year university' (p. 211). Pick out her apocalyptic hallucinations and discuss the extent to which they are 'fear' or 'fantasy' (p. 214). When thinking about them as 'fears', focus on what they suggest she will be *escaping from*. Equally, when considering them as 'fantasies', what do they suggest an *escape to*?

SECTION 3 (pp. 219–27)

Focus on: hands

INTERPRET . . .

— 'Sometimes she has to restrain an impulse to get up, cross the aisle, sit down, take hold of these alien hands' (p. 221). Look at the story of the girl whose hand is caught in the back of the 'streetcar' (pp. 219–21). Think about the way Atwood employs 'hands' in this section. How are they used to suggest connection and separation, both physically and emotionally?

RELATE THE PART TO THE WHOLE . . .

— When you have developed some ideas about the treatment of 'hands' as links in this story, extend your analysis to the collection as a whole. How do 'hands' – both thematically and linguistically – link the stories together? Which stories 'hold hands' with one another thematically? For example, refresh your memory about thematic concerns that surface again and again, such as the theme of childhood and growing up – how is this story connected with 'Hurricane Hazel', and how does nature connect both stories to the 'Scarlet Ibis' or 'Spring Song of the Frogs'?

IN SEARCH OF THE
RATTLESNAKE PLANTAIN
SECTION I (pp. 229–40)

Focus on: the theme of family

EXAMINE THE VOCABULARY . . .

— Taking the story as a whole, highlight the use of a familial vocabulary in this story. How does Atwood use 'my mother' and 'we' to construct a tight family unit in this story? Think about 'Joanne': is she a member of the family? In what ways does Atwood employ the character of Joanne to construct the 'we' that is the group from which she is excluded?

EXTEND . . .

— When you have thought about the vocabulary of the family, consider how their collective knowledge, or 'memory', is used to cement that unit. You might like to compare this to your analysis of memory in 'Spring Song of the Frogs'.

Focus on: the theme of ageing

COMPARE . . .

— 'We're looking for it because this isn't the whole story. The reason I can't remember isn't creeping senility' (p. 232). Compare the treatment of the bog's disappearance (pp. 231–2) with the account of her father's increasing ill-health. How do the two themes interweave to establish the theme of ageing? For example, compare the disappearance of different forms of moisture in both parts of the story. (Her father is described as 'turning into a raisin' (p. 239) just as the bog is seen to be drying up.)

THE SUNRISE
SECTION I (pp. 241–51)

Focus on: gender – looking at/being looked at

CONSIDER . . .

— 'Yvonne follows men' (p. 241). In this narrative Atwood spends two paragraphs setting up a particular version of Yvonne. How is her behaviour set up as 'unfeminine'? (Focus on Al and Judy's conversations about Yvonne. Think about how Atwood uses them as a mouthpiece for expectations of women, and about Yvonne's deviation from the norm (pp. 249–50).)

— How are the reader's expectations jolted when we are informed that she is an 'Artist'? Think about the ways in which the idea of Yvonne as an artist reworks who conventionally does 'the looking' and who is 'looked at'.

EXTRAPOLATE . . .

— Take this binary of looking/being looked at and consider it, first in relation to the story as a whole and then to the entire collection. Which stories immediately spring to mind? Think about how being looked at makes you into an 'object', or 'objectifies' you. What other characters are objectified (Ed in 'Bluebeard's Egg', for example)?

SECTION 2 (pp. 251–61)

Focus on: silence

ANALYSE . . .

— 'Judy sticks the envelope carefully behind the wall telephone in the kitchen; she doesn't know it's empty' (p. 251). Analyse the treatment of silence in this section of the text. How does Yvonne manipulate silence (or absence, if you wish

99

to extend the analysis) here? How do different characters 'read' her silences? Think about this, particularly in the discussion of secrets (pp. 255–6). How do silences – and by extension secrets and absences – play a central role in this story?

CONTRAST AND RE-EVALUATE . . .

— Go back to 'Bluebeard's Egg': the myth and the short story. Reconsider the construction of 'secrets' by comparing their treatment in both stories. To what extent are they treated as productive, or even necessary to the impetus of the stories? (For example, the role of the Egg is secret, but is a symbol of growth and life.) Or do you read them as the encapsulation of inexpressible horror? (For example, the murdered wives, or Yvonne's razor blade [p. 260].)

— How does this analysis help you re-evaluate your attitude to the myth referred to in the collection's title?

Focus on: the theme of the artist

CHARACTERISE . . .

— Tease out Atwood's treatment of what it means to be an 'Artist' here. How do the men she encounters read her status as an 'Artist'? Go back to your analysis of the earlier section of the story: how does her gender impact upon this characterisation, both in her perception of herself and in terms of the men she paints?

RETURNING TO THE THEME . . .

— How does Atwood revisit here a thematic consideration from earlier in the collection? (Think particularly about 'Loulou; or, The Domestic Life of the Language'.)

UNEARTHING SUITE
SECTION 1 (pp. 263–72)

Focus on: narrative shape

SELECT AND INTEGRATE . . .

— Scan this opening section for references to the previous stories – for example, compare the opening of the first story with this final one. Equally, consider the impact of phrases like 'Not for the first time it occurs to me that I could not have been born, like other people, but must have been hatched out of an egg' (p. 263). How do these references serve to bring the collection together as a whole?

— Pay particular attention to the ways in which this opening section parallels the opening story. Is the narrator the same person? How does this help to bind the stories thematically?

SECTION 2 (pp. 272–81)

Focus on: movement versus stasis

DESCRIBE AND CONSIDER . . .

— Detail the various types of movement in this section – for example, the intrepid swimming in the freezing lake (pp. 277–8). Think about how this is contrasted with the narrator's discussion of stasis.

— Consider how the movement in the story suggests the reader's movement through the different texts. What role does stillness have to play in the story?

DISCUSS . . .

— Get together in a group and talk about your understanding of the verb 'to read'. Is 'reading' a 'moving' or active pastime, or would you characterise it in terms of stillness? Think about this in terms of the narrator's attitude to movement and stillness.

Focus on: the theme of secrets

INTERPRET AND LINK . . .

— 'What is my mother's secret?' (p. 272). Once again the text focuses on the theme of secrets. Look here at the narrator's relationship to telling her mother's 'secret'. Is it treated as sufficient explanation?

— When you have delineated this final section's relationship to the 'secret', think about the whole collection's relationship to secrets, just as you may have examined 'silences' in the previous story. Focusing on the theme of secrets, forge links between the different stories. How are they connected by this thematic concern?

Looking back over the whole book

QUESTIONS FOR DISCUSSION OR ESSAYS

1. Would it matter if you read the stories out of sequence, and if so, why?

2. How do the first and last stories, 'Significant Moments in the Life of My Mother' and 'Unearthing Suite', frame the collection?

3. Do any stories occupy a special place in this collection, particularly in relation to the Bluebeard myth?

4. 'Unearthing Suite' is a joke rhyme with 'Birthing Suite'. Consider the theme of birth in any or all of the stories in this collection.

Contexts, comparisons and complementary readings

BLUEBEARD'S EGG

Focus on: oral history and folk narrative

EXPLORE CONNECTIONS . . .

Atwood's stories in *Bluebeard's Egg* exploit two traditions: that of oral history – often handed down between women – and that of the fairy-tale genre. Useful books that work with similar themes might include Alice Walker's *In Search of Our Mothers' Gardens* (1983), especially the title essay, which deals with the creative inheritance that she derives from her mother, but which also plays with the terms of oral history.

Helen Simpson's collection of short stories, *Hey Yeah Right Get a Life* (2000), is about a group of women living in a suburb of London, but sharing similar concerns about family and work.

Angela Carter's *The Bloody Chamber* (1979) is a collection of short stories that revise and re-interpret folk tales and fairy stories with a modern perspective.

Focus on: poetry and prose

SEARCH AND ANALYSE . . .

Atwood is a well known poet, as well as a prose author. Read one of her collections of poetry, such as *The Circle Game* (1967), or *The Journals of Susannah Moodie* (1970), *Morning in the Burned House* (1995), or *Eating Fire: Selected Poems 1965–1995* (1996). Seek out poems that in theme or subject matter might match any of the stories in *Bluebeard's Egg*. Then look for two things. Firstly, try to find similar uses of vocabulary, or places where Atwood uses the same word in a poem and in a prose story. Then secondly find places in the prose where she has used conventionally 'poetic' forms, such as assonance, rhythm, rhyme, alliteration and repetition. Think about the ways in which Atwood adapts her poetic technique to her prose method.

Focus on: Canadian literature

COMPARE . . .

Atwood is an important writer, but she is also an important Canadian writer. Read other Canadian authors, such as Alice Munro or Margaret Laurence. Or you might read Atwood's own book on Canadian literature, *Survival: A Thematic Guide to Canadian Literature* (1972). Or you might read a very famous Canadian book, L.M. Montgomery's *Anne of Green Gables* (1908). What specifically 'Canadian' themes can you find that appear in these books and in Atwood's short stories?

Focus on: the Gothic

RESEARCH . . .

Look up the term 'Gothic' in a glossary of literary terms, or in a *Companion to English Literature*. Some of the earliest Gothic novels were written by women like Ann Radcliffe and Mary Shelley. Think about why it might be that the genre is one that particularly appeals to women. If you read the entry on Gothic from *The Feminist Companion* edited by Virginia Blain, Patricia Clements and Isobel Grundy (Batsford, London, 1990) you will see that the several features are mentioned such as: secret and hidden places (caves, tunnels, cellars), the flow of blood, locked rooms, an emphasis on the body and on the feelings, and an element of sexual threat. Make a list of as many items as you can and consider which might be labelled 'female' in character. Then look carefully through all of the stories in Atwood's collection *Bluebeard's Egg* and see how many examples of these elements you can find, and in which stories.

Focus on: artists and the Muse

SEARCH AND COMPARE . . .

Several of the stories in *Bluebeard's Egg* are to do with the relationship between the artist and his or her Muse. Find out about the nine Muses that figure in Greek mythology. Then find out how a 'Muse' functions in inspiring an artist. Consider how these relate to any of the stories in the collection.

Focus on: food

INTERPRET AND ASSESS . . .

Many of the stories in this collection deal with food, and the preparation, cooking and eating of food. Why do you think this is? Compare some passages about food: that on p. 65 'Loulou; or The Domestic Life of the Language' with that on pp. 100–101 in 'Uglypuss', for instance. Then look at a 'lifestyle' cookbook – Nigella Lawson's *How to be a Domestic Goddess* (Chatto and Windus, London, 2000) for example – and assess the ways in which food is used to tell stories about people and the way they live a) in Atwood's stories and b) in recipe books.

VINTAGE
LIVING
TEXTS

The Blind Assassin

IN CLOSE-UP

Reading guides for

THE BLIND ASSASSIN

BEFORE YOU BEGIN TO READ . . .
— Look at the interview with Atwood. You will see that she mentions there a number of themes and techniques that are present in this novel, including:

- The question of first, third or second person
- Memory
- Freedom
- Time
- Storytelling and the novel
- Forms of fiction, including science-fiction fantasy
- Social inequalities.

DISCUSS . . .
— When you have reached the end of the novel, come back and discuss how Atwood has confirmed or complicated your expectations.

PART I, (pp. 3–8)

Focus on: openings

CONSIDER AND COMPARE . . .
'Ten days after the war ended, my sister Laura drove a car [off a] bridge' (p. 3). Think about the impact of this opening [sentence: to what extent does its concern frame the crux of [the nov]el? Think about other opening sentences, either in com[parison] with Atwood's other novels or in relation to famous [opening] lines.

[Now] compare the opening line with the news headlines [that make] up much of the narrative. Does Atwood's opening [line re]ad like a news headline? Draw out the differences [clearly] and discuss their implications.

Focus on: the theme of ambiguity

[RESEARCH] AND INTERPRET . . .
[Choose e]xamples of textual ambiguity in this opening sec[tion. For exam]ple, Iris says, 'Ten days after the war ended' [which is cl]early a specific reference to an assumed knowl[edge,] but it is not clear from this chapter which 'war' [it is.] When you have chosen examples of the text's [ambiguity think] about how they represent the thematic con[cerns.] How do these ambiguities at the opening of [the novel lead the re]ader to make assumptions? In what ways do [they affect the relati]onship between the narrator and the reader?

these headings to those of writers like George Eliot who
their titles to indicate the substance of the chapter. Doe
parallel Atwood's use of titles? If not, think about how *A*
does employ these headings? What do they foregroun
reader?

Focus on: *themes*

LIST AND EVALUATE . . .
— Think about the number of 'texts' you co
book. How many 'novels' form the body o
— List the kinds of 'texts' you encounte
way through the novel, such as newspaper
oirs and stories — both told and transcri
acterise these differences? What expe
specific kinds of texts? For example
newspaper article differently from
list as you progress through the
tions in mind. Return to them w
your way through the text.

Reading activities: detailed analysis

Focus on: *titles*

ASSESS . . .
— This novel has a great many 'titles'. Map out the occur-
rences of 'The Blind Assassin' in the titled sections, and look
at where it is printed in the body of the text. How does your
understanding of the title alter as you trace through the sections devoted to 'The Blind Assassin'?
— As you are reading, note down the links between the two
sections — what words are used to link them?
— Think about how 'The Blind Assassin' chapters form a
separate narrative within the text. Could you read them sepa-
rately from Iris's sections? How would reading the novel in a
different order change the shape of the novel?
— Consider the inclusion of an index in the novel. How might
this alter your reading of the text? What does it suggest to
you, the reader, about the text as a whole?
— Come back to these questions when you have studied the
novel and see how you would reassess your original
interpretations.

EXAMINE . . .
— Look at the individual section headings. Do they offer you
a guide to the action of the novel? You might like to compare

EVALUATE . . .
— Before beginnin
section, think abc
sections. Part I i
tive, a newspap
'The Blind A
indicate the
set up the

CO
—
off a
senten
the no
parison
opening
— Also
that make
sentence n
you identif

DISTINGUISH
— Pick out e
tion. For exan
(p. 3). This is c
edge of 'the' wa
she is referring to
ambiguities, think
cerns of the novel
the text force the r
they presume a relat

— Focus on particular instances of ambiguity within the text. Either choose from some of the examples of ambiguity picked out here, and think about their centrality to the novel, or work with another example that you find engaging. Issues:

- Laura's death
- The paternity of Iris's child
- The identity of the hero and heroine of 'The Blind Assassin'.

EXPAND . . .

— When you have interpreted the thematic ambiguity of the events of this opening section, think about the final paragraphs (pp. 4–5). How does the refusal to be clear about the 'note-books' Iris finds, or about who 'Reenie' is, link the opening three parts of Part I together? Think about how the ambiguities or 'elisions' link different sections together throughout the text.

Focus on: narrative style and tone

DESCRIBE AND EXPLORE . . .

— This second section of the novel (p. 6) is presented as an excerpt from a 'real' newspaper. Pick out the ways in which the narrative style is different from the first-person narration of the opening section.

— Then, with the close analysis you have just performed on this section, think about the following questions:

- Who is speaking?
- To whom are they speaking?
- Are you their direct audience? If not, what difference does the layering have upon your reading?

Throughout the novel you will encounter sections of newspaper 'reprinted'. Try and keep some of these issues in mind when considering their treatment as a whole.

Focus on: the theme of authorship

REFLECT . . .

— This is the opening chapter of Laura's novel (pp. 7–8). What impact does Atwood's decision to put Laura's name on the opening page have? Think about the relationship of Laura as the 'author' of this text to 'The Blind Assassin's' protagonist. Do you read Laura as the 'she' in the opening section?

DISCUSS . . .

— Keeping to this opening part, discuss the relationship of Laura as the object of Iris's narrative to this part where she is the 'author'. Bear in mind questions such as:

- How many authors have you encountered so far? (Don't forget to include the writer of the article that Atwood places between Laura and Iris.)
- How does signing your name to a story guarantee that it belongs to you?
- What difficulties does authorship present for the reader? Do you consider this to be Atwood's story in the same way that you might read 'The Blind Assassin' as Laura's?

Come back to these questions as you work your way through the text.

Focus on: metaphor and description

SELECT AND EXAMINE . . .

— Much of this section is devoted to Laura's description of a photograph. Think about the difficulties of describing images here. Pick out the phrases that you find particularly evocative and examine what it is that they suggest in detail. For example, how do phrases such as 'blown cloud in the brilliant sky, like ice cream smudged on chrome' (p. 8) work on more than one sensory level, playing on taste as well as vision?

ATTEMPT . . .
— Pick some photographs and attempt, individually, to construct metaphors to describe detailed elements of the photograph, as the narrator does here.

COMPARE . . .
— Get together in a group and compare the metaphors you have produced, thinking about the contrasting versions of the photographs you have created. How does your perception of the image alter when you hear different versions of it?

CONSIDER . . .
— Think about the consequences of your different perspectives: how do your different metaphors create different versions of the photograph itself? Then return to Iris's opening section and consider it as a discussion of perspective. How do the two women set up different versions of the events that the novel deals with in this opening section?

PART II, (pp. 11–40)

Focus on: the theme of knowledge

LIST AND ANALYSE . . .
— In Part II the reader is given various kinds of 'information'. List the different references; think about the different formats that Atwood uses here. For example, what kind of

'knowledge' do the chapters that are excerpts from 'The Blind Assassin' give the reader? As you construct your list, bear in mind the following categories:

- **Character** How do the exchanges between the unnamed hero and heroine of 'The Blind Assassin' help to construct these characters (pp. 31–3, 37–8)?
- **Context** Explore Atwood's creation of various fictional 'worlds', the communities to whom the newspapers write (pp. 17–18, 24, 30 and 39–40). Or the science-fiction location of the people of the planet Zycron (pp. 12–15, 25–8 and 33–7).
- **Plot** Think about how this section gives the reader crucial information for the development of the narrative. How do the newspaper articles work in this respect? What kind of 'knowledge' is withheld?

INTERPRET . . .

— How does Atwood play with the idea of 'knowledge' in the section as a whole, given your detailed focus upon elements of Part II?

— Consider how the section functions to move the narrative forward in terms of plot and familiarity with character; but also think about how 'knowledge' is addressed thematically. In order to develop your analysis, think about the different versions of 'knowledge' as a sexual and emotional state. Here you might particularly like to focus on 'The Blind Assassin', both in terms of the couple and the discussion of sexual and emotional relationships on Zycron.

PART III, (pp. 43–126)

Focus on: the theme of ageing

DETAIL AND ANALYSE . . .

— Pay particular attention to the opening story of Part III, 'The presentation' (pp. 43–51), and to 'The silver box' (pp. 52–9) and explore the way in which the theme of ageing is treated in these two stories. Look at the metaphors and the parallels of dying vegetation that Atwood employs (p. 43) and at Iris's discussion of how an understanding of her age has altered her perception of the world around her. For example, think about her discussion of the young girls at 'the presentation', or focus on Iris's visit to Laura's graveside (pp. 55–9).

EXPAND . . .

— When you have detailed the linguistic and thematic treatment of ageing here, think about how this is an overriding concern of the novel. To what extent is it linked to the discussion of memory or authorship, for example? Tease out its relationship to other themes you have identified in the novel.

DISCUSS . . .

— When you have had a chance to consider your attitude to the questions raised in relating different themes, get into groups to discuss your responses. Do you find ageing to sum up the book's focus more aptly than memory? This would be an interesting place for you to start a debate bringing in your different readings of the text's thematic priorities.

REASSESS . . .

— When you have extended your discussion thematically, return to the opening sections of the other chapters in Part III. To what extent do Iris's attitudes change your position on the thematic importance of ageing? You might like to return to this debate as you work your way through the text. In what ways do your responses to the issue of 'ageing' shift when you have read the text as a whole?

Focus on: the theme of personal versus public histories

EXAMINE . . .

— Focus upon the chapters entitled 'The button factory' (pp. 60–9), 'The trousseau' (pp. 82–92) and 'The gramophone' (pp. 93–102). Think about the treatment of public histories in these three chapters. For example, compare the excerpt quoted from a newspaper (p. 63) referring to industrialisation with Iris's version of her own personal encounter with 'the button factory'.

RESEARCH AND EXPLORE . . .

— Both 'The trousseau' and 'The gramophone' deal with the First World War. Atwood narrates this both from a personal and from an historical perspective. Research Canada's attitude to the war and then ponder the issues that your exploration has raised. For instance:

- Discuss Atwood's personalising of a public history. How does she achieve this?
- To what extent does the narrative of Laura and Iris's grand-parents become 'representative' – i.e. is it *de*personalised by its relationship to a bigger historical narrative?
- Does history become more 'meaningful' or 'accessible' when it is told through a focus on one family?

You may want to explore one of these questions in depth or to consider their relationship to one another.

Focus on: the theme of reading and writing

INTERPRET . . .
— Taking the part as a whole, think about Atwood's discussion of 'writing'. At various points specific writing styles are introduced and discussed: for example in 'Avilion' Iris quotes Tennyson (p. 76), or look at the 'reader' Iris is playing with in 'Bread day' (pp. 100–1). Taking these examples, interpret Atwood's employment of reading and writing in Part III. Is reading a sophisticated pastime? Is understanding clearly separated from reading in this part? How does Iris's childhood 'reader' complicate the idea of 'understanding' and how is it used to differentiate between Laura and Iris (pp. 100–1, 110)?

EXTEND . . .
— In 'Bread day' (pp. 103–17) and 'Black ribbons' (pp. 118–21) Iris talks about the importance of 'writing' as she discusses graffiti. How does she outline her approval of graffiti as a form of communication? To what extent is the ability to 'read' and 'write' presented as a fundamental here? Does Iris provide a definitive version of the power of writing in the novel in this part?

PART IV, (pp. 129–62)

Focus on: the theme of appearance

DETAIL AND ANALYSE . . .
— Look at the first of the four elements of this section (pp. 129–32) and concentrate your attention on the disagreement that the two unnamed protagonists have about the woman's appearance. Detail these differences: how is her appearance marked as being 'different'? Think both about her

physical attributes and about 'appearance' as linked to ideas about behaviour.

— When you have combed through 'The café' (pp. 129–32) looking for these particular references, think about how these differences in 'appearance' highlight the characters' opposed political stance. Consider how the narrator draws attention to differences in their clothing – for example, compare the opening of the section, with references to her 'cream-coloured' coat (p. 129) and raincoat with the closing line of 'The café': 'I know you do, he says. Girls with coats like yours do have those wishes' (p. 132). Who are the 'girls' he is thinking of?

— Analyse these differences and ask yourself:

- Are these people of the same class? If not, how is this demonstrated in their interchange?
- Is their argument 'political'? If so, what political differences can you extract from the text here?

As you continue to read the 'Blind Assassin' chapters, keep the idea of a conflict of 'appearances' in mind. How does it resurface – for example, in their attitudes to the appearance of sexuality in 'The chenille spread' (pp. 135–9)?

Focus on: historical context

RESEARCH . . .

— Look at the two newspaper articles in this section, 'The Port Ticonderoga Herald and Banner' (pp. 133–4) and 'The Mail and Empire' (pp. 140–1). These newspaper 'cuttings' make very specific reference to political issues that dominate the novel's setting. The novel uses newspapers to 'headline' the historical moment in which the novel is set.

— Use the articles as a springboard to discovering what particular events the novel introduces here. Start with broad questions, such as: what is the international economic crisis now called? How is it linked to the Wall Street Crash of 1929, for example? When you have done some general research, either in the library or through discussion, find out what the 'national crisis' (p. 133) is to which Elwood Murray refers in his editorial.

— Then research the particular terms used in the newspapers. For example, what is a 'lock-out' (p. 133)? What and where were the 'Union riots' (p. 134)? What is 'Section 98' (p. 140)? Who is Mr Roosevelt (p. 141)?

DEVELOP . . .

— When you have conducted your research, think about the dates of the two articles. How does the passage of two years influence your understanding of them? What difference does it make that one is a 'local' paper, and you are given the writer's name, and the other is an anonymous piece in a national paper?

— Consider the impact that your research has had on your understanding of the novel up until this point. Does it encourage you to consider the Chase family in a more sympathetic light? Think about how your increased awareness of the historical context of the novel affects your reading.

PART V, (pp. 165–300)

Focus on: the theme of growing up

SELECT AND EXAMINE . . .

— In the first half of Part V the focus of the narrative is upon Laura and Iris's maturation. Choose one of the girls and think about the treatment of their 'growing up' or adolescence in this section. Pick out the instances that most clearly demonstrate a shift from childhood innocence to a more adult awareness — for example, Laura's invitation to Alex Thomas at the end of 'The button factory picnic' (p. 218). Or Iris's attempt at smoking in the same chapter (p. 216–17). Extend your examination of the character you have chosen by selecting those incidents you regard to be formative.

COMPARE AND CONTRAST . . .

— When you have formulated your understanding of Atwood's treatment of adolescence, extend your analysis by comparison with someone else's response to the same task. How does your collation differ? Why do you regard different events as formative in terms of either Laura or Iris?

— Then introduce the character you did not focus upon. Compare and contrast the sisters' encounters with adulthood here. For example, you could compare Iris's relationship to poetry (p. 189) with Laura's treatment of 'Miss Violence' (pp. 185–95). Or you could look at both sisters' interaction with their father or Callie. At this point extend your material to take in all of Part V. How does Alex form the crux of both Laura and Iris's sexual and emotional maturity?

Focus on: language and style, the use of italics

DESCRIBE AND INTERPRET . . .

— Read through the first half of Part V (pp. 165–218) and pick out the instances of italics. For example, Iris's quoting of Reenie 'Never mind . . . You'll know when you're older' (pp. 167). Or in Iris's reciting of her concerns: 'I was tired of keeping an eye on Laura, . . . – but I was needed at home. Needed at home, needed at home – it sounded like a life sentence' (p. 211). While noting their usage, consider: who is speaking? Who is being spoken to? Is it the past or the present tense?

— When you have made a detailed examination and described

Atwood's use of italicisation, survey your own responses and interpret how she is employing them. For example:

- Are the italics being used to imply secrets, or topics that cannot be discussed openly?
- Do they form the subtext of conversation?
- To what extent are they used to complicate or undermine the overt discourse?
- Do they relate to Iris's memories and thus signify two conversations happening simultaneously?

DEVELOP . . .
— When you have had a chance to develop your arguments as to Atwood's employment of this literary device, extend your analysis to consider Part V as a whole. As an overall question, consider whether or not the use of italics parallels the idea of dual narratives established by the parallel narration of both Laura's and Iris's stories throughout the novel.

PART VI, (pp. 303–41)

Focus on: the language of gossip

EVALUATE . . .
— In the section entitled 'Mayfair, 1936' (p. 332) the headline is 'Toronto High Noon Gossip' (p. 332). Consider the idea of 'gossip'. Think about what you understand 'gossip' to mean. Is this reinforced in the article? What does the article consist of here, and in what respect is it commonly understood to be 'gossip'?
— Now evaluate the differences between 'gossip' and 'news'. How are the two differentiated here? (For example, think about the use of humour in the title: how is 'High Noon' made comic

by the epithet 'Gossip'). Pick out the details of the article that set it at odds with the previous article in Part V, the 'Toronto Star' section (pp. 314–15). How is one 'serious'? Be specific about the phrases that highlight these differences for you. For example, how does detailed reference to clothing on p. 322 set a different tone from the opening reference to the 'Police' (p. 314)?

EXTEND . . .

— Expand your discussion of 'gossip' to consider the gendering of the term. To what extent is it presented here as a 'female' concern? What are the thematic and linguistic pointers that might lead you to consider it to be 'female', as opposed to the 'male' focus on 'news' and serious coverage? In order to extend your analysis look at the 'Mayfair' articles in other parts (IV, for example) and contrast them with the other journalistic segments. How are your initial responses supported by looking at the articles as a group?

DISCUSS . . .

— You might like to discuss the ideas raised by this consideration of the language of gossip as 'female'. How is it used to undermine or trivialise the 'female' voice here? How is the distinction maintained, both in terms of 'female' topics and language?

Focus on: the theme of the 'clandestine'

DESCRIBE AND DISCUSS . . .

— Look at the description of the couple's meeting in 'The Blind Assassin: the houndstooth suit' (pp. 303–7). How does the text build up the detail of their erotic anticipation of seeing each other? For instance, how does the narration of her journey and his nervous waiting in 'the slut's' room (p. 306) reinforce the 'clandestine' nature of their relationship? Describe how the narrator's description of their surroundings establishes the secrecy of their relationship as being definitive to it.

— Discuss the extent to which the couple's trepidation and secrecy enhance or undermine the romance of their meeting. Do you regard the 'clandestine' as being fundamental to the attraction, or is it something the characters have to overcome? Is it a romantic obstacle, as opposed to the seduction itself?

— Think about an event in your life that you would describe as 'clandestine'. Then compare your attitudes to the 'encounter' with those you have read in the novel.

PART VII, (pp. 345–413)

Focus on: description and sense of place

COMPARE AND CONTRAST . . .

— Iris's honeymoon trip to London, Paris, Rome and Berlin is set out here, but her memories of those cities are framed by the present-day visit that she makes to her old home in Toronto, where she once lived with Richard. Compare the narrative methods used for the European cities with that used to describe the Toronto house. Make notes on the different accounts of the physical details relating to these places. How do these details about things and scenes help to portray Iris's moods: firstly, as an eighteen-year-old and, secondly, as an old lady?

Focus on: plot structure

EVALUATE . . .

— On p. 367 we are told about the many telegrams that Richard receives while he and Iris are abroad on honeymoon. Do you suspect anything? If so, why? If not, why not? Now look at p. 375 where the telegrams are explained. Consider and evaluate the dramatic impact of this explanation. Later on in the novel you will find that another telegram arrives for Iris (pp. 570–1). When you reach that section, look back at this section and consider the connections between the two episodes.

LIST . . .

— By the time you reach this section you have been given quite a bit of information about the very early days of Iris's marriage after she and Richard have returned from Europe. Remember that some of this information is told you in the sections set in the past; some of it comes from the sections that deal with Iris's memories; and some of it from the interspersed newspaper cuttings. Try to write down the strict chronological order of events. Start with Iris's and Richard's return, than add in everything that you know happens to Iris, to Laura and to Alex Thomas. What is the literary effect achieved by the fact of these pieces of information being given to us *not* in chronological order?

Focus on: key words

ASSESS . . .

— Of Richard's explanation for his behaviour, Iris remembers only six key words: '*Worry. Time. Ruined. Selfish. Forgive me*' (p. 377). Consider and assess how you might apply these words to Laura, to Iris and Laura's father, to Alex Thomas, and – but only once you have read to the end of the novel – to Iris herself.

RESEARCH AND COMPARE . . .

— Iris remembers going to a ball with the theme of 'Xanadu', taken from Samuel Taylor Coleridge's poem 'Kubla Khan' (1816). Read and research Coleridge's poem. In what ways do the themes and settings of the poem suggest parallels with the settings and events in any of the episodes in *The Blind Assassin* (not necessarily just this one)?

PART VIII, (pp. 417–43)

Focus on: the theme of storytelling

JUSTIFY . . .

— This part switches between different settings, times and written forms: from the present in the 1930s (which we are to understand is an excerpt from Laura Chase's famous novel); to the story told within the story about the goings-on on the planet Zycron; to a newspaper report about social events; back to the present (Iris on the cruise); to the memory of a past and the story of the Peach Women; to a political report in a newspaper; and back to the Zycron story within the story. Work out how each of these sections relates thematically to the others and explain the connections. Make a grid of overlapping places and times if you need to.

Focus on: point of view

ANALYSE . . .

— The girl in the 1930s story is beginning to take over the narrative of the Zycron story, or to make a bid to do so. Look at the tussle over this between the lovers. Concentrate on the criticism that each offers to the other about their vocabulary (e.g. on pp. 420 and 421) and about their respective attempts at plotting. Now consider their different agendas. What does she say about the 'undead' women on p. 422? What does he say about the social betrayal and resulting massacres involved in her plot on p. 422? How do their separate agendas relate to: a) the story being told in Laura Chase's novel, and b) the story being told about Iris's life?

Focus on: point of view and the reader's responsibility

ACCOUNT FOR . . .

— The lover in the 1930s story considers how deliciously 'luscious' and 'plumped' his beloved seems (p. 442). When he asks her to leave, she thinks that she can't because 'There's another reason too' (p. 443). What do you think the link might be? What is the reason?

PART IX, (pp. 447–86)

Focus on: characterisation

DISCRIMINATE . . .

— Iris tells certain things about her present existence as an old lady, and other things about her past existence as the wealthy and pampered wife of Richard Griffen. How do these two episodes in her life relate to one another? Can you trace the development of her character from one to the other?

Focus on: characterisation and figurative language

INTERPRET . . .

— On p. 455 Iris says, 'I was sand, I was snow – written on, rewritten, smoothed over.' She is talking about the bruises that Richard inflicts on her, but the metaphor is larger than that. On p. 461 Iris complains to Laura about her having forged her handwriting to play truant from school, saying, 'Handwriting is a personal thing. It's like stealing.' On p. 477 Iris describes Laura wearing her own old cast-off dress from last summer, and she says, 'Seeing her from behind gave me a peculiar sensation, as if I were watching myself.' Taking these images and metaphors together, what can you guess at about the relationship between Laura and Iris?

— As you continue to read, look out for other references to writing, to scripts, to forgery, to impersonation. If you look ahead to p. 498 you will find an example: 'She feels heavy and soiled, like a bag of unwashed laundry. But at the same time flat and without substance. Blank paper, on which – just discernible – there's the colourless imprint of a signature, not hers.'

— When you have finished the whole novel, look back at these images and interpret their figurative relationship to the plot and the metaphors of the book as a whole.

PART X, (pp. 489–505)

Focus on: vocabulary and word choice

DEFINE AND COMPARE . . .

— Several different types of language and vocabulary are used in these discrete passages. Look first at the opening paragraphs on p. 489, as the narrator describes the character of her search for the Lizard Men story. Jot down the different types of verb used to describe her search. Then look at p. 492 and the reverie on the word 'unhinged'. These passages are narrated by someone interested in the effects and power of words as images.

— Now set those passages against the two newspaper reports in this part. How does the language of society gossip (p. 494 on) compare with the language of authority in Witherspoon's letter (p. 496 on)?

— Next, set each of those examples against the vocabulary that characterises the two passages entitled 'The tower' (p. 498

on) and 'Union Station' (p. 503 on). How do you know that each of these is couched in the language of romance? Find examples (words and phrases) of that language.

Focus on: *narrative connections*

ASSESS . . .

— If you turn to the interview with Atwood you will see that she speaks about the colour imagery in the 'pulp science fiction' sections of this novel. Now compare the use of colour in the two passages called 'The tower' and 'Union Station'. Assess why it might be that colour is used so vividly in these two passages. Make a case for this narrative connection.

PART XI, (pp. 509–551)

Focus on: *the theme of relationships and storytelling*

EXAMINE AND CONTRAST . . .

— As the novel gathers towards its conclusion, and the plot towards its resolution, Iris enquires rhetorically of her imagined reader, 'Was I my sister's keeper?' (p. 522). Consider the respective relationships between Iris and Laura, Iris and Aimée and Sabrina, Iris and Winifred, Iris and Reenie, Iris and Myra. Iris is the connector here. But what about the relationships between Winifred and Laura, or Reenie and Laura, or Winifred and Aimée? Are they – any of them – 'their sister's keeper'?

— In the light of the larger issues around this question of responsibility and manipulation, you might also look at some of the stories in Atwood's collection *Bluebeard's Egg,* especially 'Significant Moments in the Life of My Mother' and 'Two Stories About Emma'. Compare the treatment of relationships between women that you find there with the treatment of the many relationships between the various women who people *The Blind Assassin*.

PART XII, (pp. 555–74)

Focus on: irony, and background and foreground

ANALYSE . . .

— In 'Yellow Curtains' the narrator of the novel within the novel imagines how she will leave and live alone on apples and soda crackers, waiting for her lover to return. She doesn't do so. 'None of this happens, of course. Or it does happen, but not so you would notice. It happens in another dimension of space' (p. 569). Then she dreams that she sees her lover and has a vision of the destruction of their fantasy city: 'It's only another dimension of space' (p. 574). Each of the short passages in this part is set in more than one 'dimension'. By now we have enough information to realise the ironies of setting what is going on in the foreground (that is, what people are doing and saying and performing) as opposed to what is going on in the background (that is, what people are thinking and feeling). Work through each chapter and make two lists: one for foreground, one for background. Then analyse the literary effect of these juxtapositions.

PART XIII, (pp. 577–603)

Focus on: characterisation

EVALUATE . . .

— The older Iris, narrating her story, says, 'I've failed to convey Richard in any rounded sense. He remains a cardboard cut-out.

I know that' (p. 585). But we are about to learn quite a bit more about him, as we are about Laura. Consider the characterisation of Laura and Richard in the novel as a whole, and assess the effect of the fact that the narrative has – until now – withheld key pieces of information about their relation to each other.

Focus on: key words

DEFINE . . .

— Iris cannot recall a word, 'escarpment', on p. 598. Consider the relevance of this word – and the various meanings of this word – to the novel as a whole. Include metaphorical significances in your list, as well as literal ones.

— Now look at the list of words that Iris repeats to herself on p. 598: 'God, Trust, Sacrifice, Justice, Faith, Hope, Love, Sister'. Analyse the significance of each of these in relation to the themes of the novel as a whole.

PART XIV, (pp. 607–27)

Focus on: the theme of memory and 'heap of rubble'

COMMENT ON . . .

— At the end of the last part we learned that Laura has said that she will talk to Iris 'later'. Iris begins to realise that Laura has left her a message. Read the passage about the contents of the doctored notebooks on pp. 608–11. There is the story of Dido and her companion Iris in *Latin*; the photograph in *History*; the note about the river at Port Ticonderoga in *Geography*; the list of arcane words that Alex had noted in *French*; and a coded list of dates in *Mathematics*. In some ways this collection of codes is a summary of the novel as a whole. Comment on each one and relate it to the events of two novels:

'The Blind Assassin' as written by Laura Chase and *The Blind Assassin* as written by Atwood.

SUMMARISE . . .

— Analyse the relationship between Laura's fragmentary communication and the city that is a 'heap of rubble': a) in the memory of the narrator in the novel within the novel, and b) in Iris's memories. If you look at the interview with Margaret Atwood earlier in this book, you will see that she discusses there a source for this episode.

ARE YOU SURPRISED? . . .

— On p. 626 Iris admits that she wrote 'The Blind Assassin' by Laura Chase. She says – to us – 'but you must have known that for some time'. Did you guess? Are you surprised by this revelation?

PART XV, (pp. 631–37)

Focus on: narrative method

COMPARE AND ACCOUNT FOR . . .

— Iris says that she was the 'bodiless hand, scrawling across a wall' (p. 626). Then we have heard the story of Laura's childish imaginings of the hierarchy in heaven and the seating arrangements, whether on the left or right hand (p. 627). Then we see again the photograph with the excised picture of Iris – only her hand left in the image, 'The hand that will set things down' (p. 631). Compare these instances of the image of the 'hand'. Think of as many common phrases as you can that include the word 'hand' (to lend a hand, to give a hand, a helping hand, to have a hand in something, to recognise someone's hand . . . there are many others.) When you have compiled your list, apply as many of these images as you can to the text of the novel as a whole. How does an image or a metaphor help to bind together a fictional narrative? Can you find any poems that exploit the image of hands? How far might it be true to say that Atwood's technique is an example of a poetic, rather than a novelistic, method?

JUSTIFY . . .

— If you look at the interview with Atwood, you will see that she speaks about the importance – from a writing point of view – of knowing who it is that your narrator is addressing. In the last chapter here Iris imagines her granddaughter Sabrina as the ideal listener, the person to whom she addresses herself. Consider and justify this choice of addressee for Iris.

Looking over the whole novel

QUESTIONS FOR DISCUSSION OR ESSAYS

1. 'The only way you can write the truth is to assume that what you set down will never be read' (p. 345). Consider Atwood's employment of the addresser and the addressee in the novel as a whole.

2. Atwood has described the narrative method of *The Blind Assassin* as 'a Chinese box'. Interpret this remark and relate it to the structure of the novel.

3. 'My fingers itched with spite. I knew what had happened next. I'd pushed her off' (p. 595). Once you have read the whole novel, ask yourself this question: how many times does Iris push Laura off?

4. 'All stories are about wolves. All stories worth repeating, that is. Anything else is sentimental drivel' (p. 423). Discuss.

5. 'It's loss and regret and misery and yearning that drive the story forward, along its twisted road' (p. 632). Consider this statement in relation to the plot and the narrative structure of *The Blind Assassin*.

6. 'Iris Chase Griffen, A Memorable Lady' (p. 633). Consider the ways in which Iris might be 'memorable': firstly in the life of Myra, and secondly in your own imagination.

7. 'But I leave myself in your hands' (p. 637). Who has been left, and in whose hands? Discuss.

Contexts, comparisons and complementary readings

THE BLIND ASSASSIN

Focus on: literary method

COMPARE AND RE-CREATE . . .

— One way of describing the literary narrative method of *The Blind Assassin* is as a 'collage'. During the 1930s – which is when part of the novel is set – this was an inventive modernist form exploited by many artists, who would take everyday and 'found' objects and juxtapose them on a canvas or in a sculpture, possibly adding paint and other such traditional materials as well, to make a 'story' in an artwork, which – partly – has to be deduced by the enquiring perspective of the viewer. Research such pictures and compare them with the method used in Atwood's novel.

— Alternatively, try making such a picture for yourself so that it coincides with the concerns of the novel.

— Or make yourself a story by cutting out newspaper reports – or inventing them – and sandwiching them with fictional passages, on the model of *The Blind Assassin*.

COMPARE . . .
Like *The Blind Assassin*, Ian McEwan's novel *Atonement* (2001)
is the story of a novel set within a novel. During the course
of reading *Atonement* we discover that much of what we have
read is 'actually' a novel, written by Briony, one of the characters in the story we are reading. *The Blind Assassin* offers a
different surprise. Compare the two novels in terms of their
exploitation of this literary device.

Focus on: the theme of glamour, brittleness and loss

COMPARE . . .
— Read F. Scott Fitzgerald's novel *The Great Gatsby* (1925).
Gatsby dies young, as Laura does. He also has a glamour about
his life, comparable to that which Laura acquires in death.
Compare and contrast the treatment of 'beautiful young things'
in the two novels. Or you might try Ernest Hemingway's *Fiesta*
(1927) or Evelyn Waugh's *A Handful of Dust* (1934), which also
portray brittle lives where social entertainment dominates and
few 'real' values obtain. Compare the picture of the lives lived
by Jay Gatsby and Tony and Brenda Last with the kinds of
lives lived by Iris and Richard and Winifred Griffen.

Focus on: genre appeal and popular culture

LOOK UP AND CONSULT . . .
— Atwood's novel *The Blind Assassin* has its own website at:
http://www.randomhouse.com/features/atwood. Look it up
and consider why it might be that this particular novel should
attract this kind of attention? Why does the fantasy element
in the novel prove so attractive to so many people?

VINTAGE
LIVING
TEXTS

Reference

Selected extracts from reviews

These brief extracts from reviews of Atwood's work are designed to be used to suggest angles on the text that may be relevant to the themes of the books, their settings, their literary methods, their historical contexts, or to indicate their relevance to issues, questions or problems today.

Sometimes one reviewer's opinion will be entirely contradicted by another's. You might use these passages to ask yourself whether or not you agree with the writer's assessments. Or else you may take phrases from these reviews to use for framing questions – for discussion, or for essays – about the texts.

The excerpts here have been chosen because they offer useful and intelligent observations. In general, though, when you are reading reviews in newspapers, it is best to remember two things: they are often written under pressure, and they have to give the reader some idea of what the book under discussion is like, so they do tend to give space to summarising the plot.

None of these critical opinions are the last word. They are simply contributions to a cultural debate. As such, they should be approached with intellectual interest – because they can give the mood and tone of a particular time – and they should be treated with caution – because the very fact of that prevailing mood and time may intervene.

Elaine Showalter
From the *New Statesman*, October 2000
On the exploitation of literary traditions

In many respects, Atwood's *The Blind Assassin* recalls her most celebrated novel, *The Handmaid's Tale*, turned inside out. The female narrator is obsessed with memory and truth, but is wildly unreliable and secretive. Atwood employs a gothic architecture of basements and attics, and a similarly gothic decor of trunks, torn photographs and elaborate costume. Her heroines are sacrificial victims legitimised by religion, myth and fairy tale: but this time, a man – the handsome young left-wing revolutionary, Alex Thomas – is the captive, hidden in the attic by the two sisters after a violent strike causes a foreman's death.

The state of female erotic thraldom, traditional in both fairy tale and pornography, is a favourite theme of Atwood's. But for her, as opposed to Angela Carter, with whom she has many affinities, the male object of fascination scarcely seems to matter. Alex in *The Blind Assassin* and Nick in *The Handmaid's Tale* are shadowy catalysts who release the woman, awakening her to her own condition.

Iris and Laura are both exceptionally sensual, especially with regard to smells and textures. They are both fascinated by Coleridge's 'Kubla Khan', and Iris dreams of dressing as the Abyssinian maiden at the Xanadu-themed society ball in Toronto in 1935. Iris's astonishing dreams reveal both her aggression and her submissiveness; she dreams that her legs are covered with hair, growing fur. Like Angela Carter's wolf-girls, Iris finds her inner wolf in erotic obsession.

Lisa Appignanesi
From the *Independent*, September 2000
On genre

Atwood has long been adept at ransacking genre fiction for her own ends. In *Bodily Harm*, it was the spy thriller; in *The Handmaid's Tale*, future fiction; in *The Robber Bride*, a chilling riff on the gothic transported to the far reaches of the sex wars; in *Alias Grace*, an astute take on the historical crime novel. In *The Blind Assassin*, her tenth novel, the genre offered for our and, one suspects, her own delectation is pulp fantasy.

This virtuoso culling of popular forms makes each of her novels a surprise. It is, however, only part of the story – nowhere more so than in this new book, where the pulp fantasy is a lovers' elaborate bedtime tale told within a posthumously published novel, entitled *The Blind Assassin*, by one Laura Chase. Laura is the dead sister of Iris, the 83-year-old narrator of Atwood's architectonic fiction, who is herself writing a memoir of lives brutally punctuated by two world wars.

Anita Brookner
From the *Spectator*, October 2000
On setting, characterisation and literary form

Retro chic is a feature of this novel, since the main action takes place at some time in the Thirties. This means tea dances, ocean liners, hats with veils, over-powering female relatives. Of the two sisters Iris is the more unfortunate: sold, virtually, to a man 20 years her senior to bolster the family's precarious fortunes, she too writes her story, the story of her sister Laura and how she brought disgrace and fame to the family.

Laura is oblique, unknowable, as is the manner of her appearance in the novel She comes onto the page as one of the voices in a confected story, a pulp science-fiction fantasy of galactic activities, the invention of an unnamed lover who eventually comes into focus. The story is his method of seduction, and is elaborated throughout several chapters. These modish intertextualities, something of a cliché in contemporary fiction, are slightly tiresome, told at too great length they risk boring the reader. This could be the case here were it not for the storyteller, who, it appears, is unreliable (but we guessed that). He is an orphan, a strike organiser, a man on the run, with access to various dirty rooms lent by friends. The blind assassin of the title features in the pulp fantasy he invents for Laura, one of a tribe of professional child-killers in that mythical kingdom which becomes more elaborate by the page. It is with a shock, the first of many, that we learn how young Laura is. Her love affair with the teller of the story might make of her an adult before her time. Simultaneously she remains the little girl, the little sister we know, or trust, her to be.

Very gradually the lover, Alex, becomes less nebu-lous, but his origins remain unclear. He lives by writing for trash magazines; he is a communist or a Bolshevik; he is all kinds of bad news. Laura's secret is not really a secret, but it is supervised by watchful adults. It is thus kept entirely secret, or would be, had it not had an unpredictable posterity. But Iris too has a secret, and although surrounded by speculation it remains unverifiable. Her awful husband, who has political ambitions and a variety of received opinions, takes care of both sisters, in his own awful way. Indeed he takes care of them so successfully that scandal is averted and reputations kept inviolate.

Kathryn Hughes
From the *Sunday Telegraph*, September 2000
On literary form

Ever attentive to the limitations and possibilities of genre, Atwood has written what passes for a sprawling family saga stretched over 500 pages. Of course, this being Atwood, nothing is quite as simple as it seems, and the outer envelope of the novel contains another novel, also called *The Blind Assassin* which, in turn, contains yet another of the same name. In addition, there are newspaper cuttings, commenting upon and qualifying the main thread of the action.

In anyone else's hands this Russian-doll effect would seem tricksy and even *passé*. But Atwood manages the shifts of tone and time brilliantly, allowing us to find our bearings before pulling the narrative rug slyly from beneath our feet.

Alex Clark
From the *Guardian*, September 2000
On literary form

In her tenth novel, Margaret Atwood again demon-
strates that she has mastered the art of creating
dense, complex fictions from carefully layered narratives, making use of an array of literary devices –
flashbacks, multiple time schemes, ambiguous, inde-
terminate plots – and that she can hook her readers
by virtue of her exceptional storytelling skills. *The
Blind Assassin* is not a book that can easily be put to
one side, in spite of its length and the fact that its
twists and turns occasionally try the patience.

Atwood has always sought to collapse and subvert
different genres, so it isn't surprising that her family
saga should encompass pulp sci-fi, clue-strewn detective novel, newspaper reportage and tragic confes-
sional romance. The ingenuity of its chameleon
narrative, and Atwood's assured handling of atmosphere, constitute an impressive attempt to cover an
awful lot of ground – not least the whirlwind of
social and political change that makes the sisters' rar-
efied childhood a dangerous anachronism – at the
same time as exploring the hidden history of one
family.

Erica Wagner
From *The Times*, September 2000
On fiction, writers and readers

There is, however, a deeper narrative truth in the
novel. The resolution of Atwood's work makes the

reader look hard at what is believed about the relationship between authors and their writing. Too often, the cult of the author moves far, far away from the writer's work, and the writer – dead, in Laura Chase's case, or the case of a writer like Sylvia Plath – cannot answer those who would speak for her. *The Blind Assassin* makes the outrageous assertion that fiction may be just that, fiction, and what is laid on the page in the shape of 'reality' may have no more – and no less – a connection to events than the pulp fiction tale of life on a distant planet. When fiction is true, it is because the emotions it evokes in the reader ring clearly in that reader's heart, not because events it relates have an equivalent in the world beyond the book's covers.

Glossary of literary terms

Allegorical An allegory is a piece of fiction that can be read on both a surface and an abstract level. Within an allegorical tale every name, place and plot development is used deliberately to structure a story that has a much deeper underlying meaning than the 'surface' story. For example John Bunyan's *The Pilgrims Progress*. In this narrative a man named Christian (who is representative of any Christain) undertakes an arduous journey from his home (earth) to the Heavenly City (Heaven) while avoiding the temptations (sins) placed in his path.

Allusions A reference within one body of literature to any other fictional or historical character, event or place. Allusions should be recognizable to the reader. For this reason, both the Bible and William Shakespeare are often alluded to due to their worldwide presence and popularity.

Anachronism When a literary reference is made to an object, event, person or thing that is completely out of place in the natural order in time. For example, in Shakespeare's *'Julias Caesar'* a clock chimes although the play takes place long before clocks were invented.

Assonance Found mostly in poetry, assonance is the close repletion of the middle vowel sounds between differing consonant sounds: i.e. m*a*de/p*a*le. An example of this can be found in Edith Sitwell's 'The Drum' 'Wh*i*nnying, n*ei*ghed the m*a*ned blue wind.'

Characterisation The way in which an author creates and then 'fleshes out' a character. Skilled fiction writers can create utterly believable characters through their choices of the characters' dress, speech and actions.

Clichés An expression that has been overused so much it has lost its original vivacity and clarity of expression. For example 'Sharp as a tack'. Any obvious or time-honoured plots, themes or characters are also considered clichéd. For example the cackling villain or the weeping heroine.

Colloquial Colloquial language refers to everyday language and conversation. A colloquialism is a word or phrase that we would normally use in conversation or informal writing but would be inappropriate in a formal essay. For example: Jessie won't *let on* but I know she had *a lot* of difficulty getting those tickets.

Comedy A literary work that seeks to amuse its audience. Usually this involves humorus situations featuring everyday characters employing ordinary language. There are however, many different forms of comedy, such as the Comedy of Manners that uses wit to ridicule social codes and pretensions of the day. or example the TV show 'Keeping up Appearances'.

Double Perspective When the authorial voice tells the reader both the actions and events of the present, and also what they feel about these events with the luxury of hindsight. For example: 'As I walked down the steps I felt excited to see him again. It was only later that I would realise how foolish I had been.'

Epic The traditional Epic form is a long narrative poem that conforms to certain literary conventions. Epic tales usually detail the exploits of a larger than life hero in a remote time and place. Epic tales were originally handed down orally to explain the myths and legends of a race or country.

Epigraph A motto or quotation that precedes a book or chapter.

Epistolary A novel written in the form of letters, usually between two or more characters.

Epithet An adjective of adjective phrase applied to a person or an object in order to emphasize a specific quality or attribute. For example: '*Lily-livered* coward'

Fable A brief and simplistic story told for the purpose of highlighting a moral lesson.

Fictional narrative An imaginary story.

Figurative Language When prose or poetry uses language that includes figures of speech such as similes, personification, metaphors and hyperbole. For example: 'The broom danced across the kitchen floor' contains personification and is therefore an example of a sentence employing figurative language.

First Person Narrator When the narrative is told through the eyes of one character, using the pronoun 'I'.

Genre A category or type of literary work, e.g. novel, short story, poem etc. Genres can also be more specific – comedy, mystery, love story, etc.

Imagery The use of words to create pictorial images. Imagery often appeals to all the senses of taste, sight, touch and sound, and works on both literal and figurative levels.

Irony The discrepancy between the appearance of a situation and its reality. Irony can be verbal – for example, when someone says, 'I'm *fine*' but means 'I'm angry'. Or situational – for example, a blind man who sells glasses. Dramatic irony is when the audience knows more than the characters.

Ironic Juxtapositions An ironic juxtaposition is when two events are placed alongside each oter with the intention of creating an ironic link between the two. For example one character may be in the bath while another is drowning at sea.

Juxtapose When one event is positioned alongside another, usually with the intention of creating a literary link between the two. For example the birth of a baby and the simultaneous breaking of a vase.

Layered Narratives When two or more different narratives or narrative points of view are available to the reader. In this way the reader is able to develop a more rounded and thorough understanding of both the plot and the characters. Layered narratives are often interwoven throughout the novel to 'plait' together different characters' lives and experiences.

Linguistics Lingistics is the study of language as a system.

Melodrama A dramatic piece characterized by sensational incident and violent appeals to the emotions, but with a happy ending.

Metaphorical/Metaphor A figure of speech that ascribes the qualities (literally or imaginatively) of one thing to another/ For example.'morning is/a new sheet of paper for you to write on' – Eve Meriam

Myth A narrative with an unknown origin that has been passed through the generations orally and attempts to explain basic features of humanity – religious beliefs, the origin or life, a natural phenomenon etc. Myths also detail the deeds of superheroes. Like fables and legends, myths are traditionally fictitious stories.

Narrative Constructions The way in which a narrative is constructed.

Narrative Framework The way in which the narrative is 'framed' or read in context to, themes that appear throughout the story.

Narrative Method The method in which the author chooses to tell the story.

Narrative Patterns The literary methods used that contribute towards the overall shape of the narrative. For example repetition can be used which can create a 'narrative pattern'.

Narrative Shape The shape in which the narrative is constructed.

Narrative Shifts When the narrative switches between different places, situations and/or characters.

Narrative Strategy The writing strategy or 'game plan' employed by an author. This determines when and how much information is given to the reader about both the characters and the plot.

Narrative Structure The way in which the narrative is structured. A story can be told chronologically, using flashbacks, beginning at the end, etc.

Narrative Styles The different narrative styles an author can use in order to manipulate the reader.

Parable A short story that contains and illuminates a moral lesson. For example the parable of the tortoise and the hare teaches the moral lesson that slow and steady wins the race.

Parallel Narration When two narrators tell their stories at the same pace throughout the novel. The differing points of view are interwoven within the novel in order to give the reader a dual perspective of the characters, actions and events.

Parody When one composition ridicules another familiar composition through imitation and exaggeration of the style, content or structure.

Pathetic Fallacy When the state of the weather matches or mimics a characters' state of mind. Also when human emotions are attributed to nature. For example in Mary Shelley's *Frankenstein* Victor Frankenstein is depressed and angry and the weather reflects this: 'The rain (was) pouring in torrents and thick mists hid the summit of the mountain'

Pejorative and Valorised Language Language used to

describe a character, place or event that is either Negative (Pejorative) or Heroic (Valorised).

Present Tense Narrative When the narrative is written in the present tense. For example: 'I sit down and sip my coffee.'

Protagonist The hero/heroine or central character of any literary work.

Proverb A short saying that contains a commonplace truth. For example: 'A friend in need is a friend indeed.'

Pun A form of wit that involves a play on a word with a double meaning. For example, in *Romeo and Juliet* when Mercutio has been stabbed he says: 'Ask for me tomorrow and you will find me a *grave* man'

Realist A realist text deals with characters and situations that are true to life. They should be familiar and appear realistic to readers. Realism is also the name of a literary movement that began in Europe during the 19th century. Writers wanted to reflect the life of an ordinary person rather than just concentrate on fantasy heroes in far off lands.

Rhetoric In both speech and literature rhetoric is the art of persuasion.

Romance A fictional work that deals with adventure, colourful characters, extravagant plot lines and exotic locations or passionate love. Today we think of a romance novel as a love story. However, there are actually two separate forms of the Romance novel. The traditional 'Popular Romance' and the 'Adventure Story' such as spy thrillers and detective stories.

Satire/Social Satire A literary technique that combines many other methods of humour such as sarcasm, wit, irony and caricature in order to create a comic effect. Usually the purpose of the satire is to illuminate the folly, vice or greed of individuals or institutions. For this reason much of satire is considered political because it seeks to not only amuse its audience but also to make them realise certain truths about society. Ali G, at the start of his career, was considered a satirist, as he was a Cambridge graduate masquerading as a Staines street youth. He simultaneously managed to make fun of or satirise, both youth culture and the establishment's treatment of young 'streetwise' adults. Social Satire specifically satirises aspects of society.

Similes A figure of speech that employs the terms *like*, *as* or *as if* to compare two different actions, objects or attributes that share something in common. For example: '. . . his brown skin hung in strips/like ancient wallpaper' Elizabeth Bishop

Speculative fiction A work of fiction that speculates what our world could be like if it were similar to what we know, yet crucially different. For example, George Orwell in *1984* speculated what life would be like if the Thought Police monitored our every idea and the government watched over us 24/7.

Stream of consciousness A method employed by a writer that attempts to recreate the inner workings of a character's mind for the reader. Punctuation and grammar may be informal and trains of thought broken in order to successfully mimic the chaos of the free-flowing mind.

Symbolise Symbolism is the use of words, characters, actions and objects that are to be understood literally but also represent higher, more abstract concepts, i.e. a caged bird can signify the literal fact of a bird in a cage as well as the symbolic values of lost freedom, feeling trapped, etc.

Theme The central or overriding idea behind the story. The theme of a novel is often thought to contain the 'message' behind the work.

Third Person When a narrator tells the story from outside the narrative, yet also from a character's perspective, i.e. Millie sat down weakly and thought, 'Well that's it then'.

Tone The attitude of the writing – be it carefree, formal, suspenseful, etc.

Tragedy A piece of fiction that traces the downfall of a protagonist who is often portrayed as being 'better' than the rest of us. The 'tragedy' is that the fall from grace is brought about through some accident, an error in judgement or a cruel twist of fate. Often it occurs because of a 'tragic flaw' within the protagonist.

Unreliable Narrator When a reader feels they cannnot entirely trust their narrator.

Biographical outline

1939 18 November: Margaret Eleanor Atwood born in Ottawa, Ontario, Canada.

1961 Attended Victoria College, University of Toronto. Awarded E. J. Pratt Medal.

1962 Attended Radcliffe College, Cambridge, Mass.

1962–3 and 1965–7 Attended Harvard University, Cambridge, Mass.

1964–5 Lecturer in English, University of British Columbia, Vancouver.

1966 Governor General's Award for *Circle Game*.

1967–8 Instructor in English, Sir George Williams University, Montreal.

1969 *The Edible Woman* published. Won the Union Poetry Prize (Chicago).

1969–70 Attended the University of Alberta.

1971–2 Assistant Professor of English, York University, Toronto.

1972–3 Writer-in-residence, University of Toronto.

1973 *Surfacing* published.

1974 Won the Bess Hoskins Prize for Poetry (Chicago).

1976 *Lady Oracle* published.

1977 Won the City of Toronto Book Award, the Periodical Distributors of Canada Short Fiction Award and the

Canadian Booksellers' Association Award.

1978 Won the St Lawrence Award for Fiction.

1980 *Life Before Man* published.

1981 Became a Companion of the Order of Canada.

1982 *Bodily Harm* and *Dancing Girls* published.

1984 *Murder in the Dark* published.

1986 *The Handmaid's Tale* published. Won the Ida Nudel Humanitarian Award, the *Los Angeles Times* Fiction Award and the Toronto Arts Award for *The Handmaid's Tale*.

1987 *Bluebeard's Egg* published. Writer-in-residence, Macquarie University, Australia. Shortlisted for the Booker Prize. Won the Arthur C. Clarke Award for Best Science Fiction and the Humanist of the Year Award. Became a Fellow of the Royal Society of Canada.

1989 *Cat's Eye* published. Shortlisted for the Booker Prize. Writer-in-residence, Trinity University, San Antonio, Texas.

1990 Awarded the Order of Ontario and the Centennial Medal, Harvard University.

1991 *Wilderness Tips* published.

1992 *Good Bones* published.

1993 *The Robber Bride* published. Won the Canadian Authors' Association Novel of the Year for *The Robber Bride*.

1994 Awarded the Government of France's Chevalier dans l'Ordre des Arts et des Lettres. Won the *Sunday Times* Award for Literary Excellence.

1996 *Alias Grace* published. Awarded the Norwegian Order of Literary Merit. Shortlisted for the Booker Prize for *Alias Grace*.

2000 *The Blind Assassin* published. Won the Booker Prize for *The Blind Assassin*.

2001 Shortlisted for the Orange Prize for *The Blind Assassin*.

Select bibliography

WORKS BY MARGARET ATWOOD

The Edible Woman (Andre Deutsch, London, 1969; Virago, 1980)

Surfacing (Andre Deutsch, 1973; Virago, 1979)

Lady Oracle (Andre Deutsch, 1977; Virago, 1982)

Life Before Man (Jonathan Cape, London, 1980; Vintage, 1996)

Bodily Harm (Jonathan Cape, 1982; Vintage, 1996)

Dancing Girls (Jonathan Cape, 1982; Vintage, 1996)

Murder in the Dark (Jonathan Cape, 1984; Virago, 1994)

The Handmaid's Tale (Jonathan Cape, 1986; Vintage, 1996)

Bluebeard's Egg (Jonathan Cape, 1987; Vintage, 1996)

Cat's Eye (Bloomsbury, London, 1989; Virago, 1990)

Wilderness Tips (Bloomsbury, 1991; Virago, 1992)

Good Bones (Bloomsbury, 1992; Virago, 1993)

The Robber Bride (Bloomsbury, 1993; Virago, 1994)

Alias Grace (Bloomsbury, 1996; Virago, 1997)

The Blind Assassin (Bloomsbury, 2000; Virago, 2001)

Survival: A Thematic Guide to Canadian Literature (Avanti, Toronto, 1972)

Negotiating with the Dead: A Writer on Writing (Cambridge University Press, 2002)

'Ophelia has a lot to answer for' http://www.web.net/owtoad/ophelia.html (January 4th 2002)

'Spotty-handed villainesses' http://www.web.net/owtoad/vlness.html

Biographical and critical studies

Ildiko de Papp Carrington, 'Definitions of Fool: Alice Munro's 'Walking on Water' and Margaret Atwood's 'Two Stories About Emma: The Whirlpool Rapids, and Walking on Water', in *Studies in Short Fiction* Vol. 28 (2), (Spring, 1991), pp. 135–149.

Ildney Cavalcanti, 'Utopias of Language in Contemporary Feminist Literary Dystopias', *Journal of the Society for Utopian Studies*, Vol. 11, part 2, (2000), pp. 152–180.

Nathalie Cooke, *Margaret Atwood, A Biography* (ECW Press, Toronto, 1998).

Pamela Cooper, 'Sexual Surveillance and Medical Authority in Two Versions of *The Handmaid's Tale*' in *Journal of Popular Culture* Vo. 28 (4), (Spring 1995), pp. 49–66

Anne Cranny-Francis, *Feminist Fiction: Feminist Uses of Generic Fiction* (Polity Press, Oxford, 1990)

F. Davey, *Margaret Atwood: A Feminist Poetics* (Talonbooks, Vancouver, 1984)

Ed. A.E. and C.N. Davidson, *The Art of Margaret Atwood: Essays in Criticism* (Anansi, Toronto, 1981)

Glen Deer, 'Rhetorical Studies in *The Handmaid's Tale*: Dystopia and the Paradoxes of Power', in *English Studies in Canada* vol. 18 (2), (June 1992), pp. 215–233.

June Deery, 'Science for Feminists: Margaret Atwood's Body

of Knowledge', in *Twentieth Century Literature: A Scholarly and Critical Journal*, Vol. 43, part 4 (Winter, 1997), pp. 440–486

Danita Dodson, '"We Lived in the Blank White Spaces": Rewriting the Paradigm of Denial in Atwood's *The Handmaid's Tale*'. in *Utopian Studies* Vol. 8, part 2 (1997), pp. 66–86.

Marta Dvorak, 'Writing Beyond the Beginning; or, Margaret Atwood's Art of Storytelling', *Commonwealth Essays and Studies* Vol. 22, part 1, (Autumn, 1999), pp. 29–35.

Lois Feuer, 'The Calculus of Love and Nightmare: The Handmaid's Tale and the Dystopian Tradition' in *Critique: Studies in Contemporary Fiction*, Vol. 32, part 2 (Winter, 1997), pp. 96–104.

Dorota Filipczak, 'Is there no Balm in Gilead?: Biblical Intertext in The Handmaid's Tale', in *Literature and Theology* vol. 7 (2), (June 1993), pp. 171–185.

Laurel J. Gardner, 'Pornography as a Matter of Power in The Handmaid's Tale', in *Notes on Contemporary Literature* Vol. 24, part 5 (November 1994), pp. 5–7.

Ronald P. Glasberg, 'The Dynamics of Domination: Levi's Survival in Auschwitz, Solzhenitsyn's *Gulag Archipelago* and Margaret Atwood's *The Handmaid's Tale*', in *Canadian Review of Comparative Literature*, Vol. 21, part 4 (December 1994), pp. 679–693.

Barbara Godard, 'Telling it Over Again: Margaret Atwood's Art of Parody', in *Canadian Poetry* vol. 21, (Fall–Winter, 1997), pp. 1–30.

Dominick M. Grace, '*The Handmaid's Tale*: "Historical Notes" and Documentary Subversion', in *Science Fiction Studies*, Vol. 25, part 3 (76), (November 1998), pp. 481–494.

David S. Hogsette, 'Margaret Atwood's Rhetorical Epilogue in *The Handmaid's Tale*: The Reader's Role in Empowering Offred's Speech Act' in *Critique: Studies in Contemporary*

Fiction, Vol. 38, part 4, (Summer 1997), pp. 262–278.

Coral Ann Howells, *Private and Fictional Worlds: Canadian Women Novalists of the 1970's and 1980's* (Methuen and Co., London, 1987)

Coral Ann Howells, *Margaret Atwood, The Handmaid's Tale*, York Notes, 1993.

Earl Ingersoll, (ed.) and Philip Howard (introd), *Margaret Atwood: Conversation* (Ontaro Review Press, Princeton, 1990).

Lee A Jacobus and Regina Barreca (eds.) *Litterature: The Margaret Atwood Issue* (December, 1995)

Brian Johnson, 'Language, Power, and Responsibility in *The Handmaid's Tale*: Towards a Discourse of Literary Gossip', in *Canadian Literature* vol. 148, (Spring 1996), pp. 39–55.

Marion Lomax, 'Gendered Writing and the Writer's Stylistic Identity', in *Essays and Studies* (vol. 47 (1994), pp. 1–19.

Judith McCombs and Carole L. Palmer (eds.) *Margaret Atwood: A Reference Guide* (G.K. Hall, Boston, MA. 1991).

Jean Mallinson, *Margaret Atwood* (ECW Press, Toronto, n.d.).

Ed. Sara Mills, Lynne Pearce, Sue Spaull and Elaine Millard, *Feminist Readings: Feminists Reading* (Harvester, Sussex, 1989).

Madonne Miner, '"Trust Me": Reading the Romance Plot in Margaret Atwood's *The Handmaid's Tale*' in *Twentieth Century Literature* Vol. 37 (2), (Summer 1991), pp. 148–168.

Janet J. Montelaro, 'Maternity and the Ideology of Sexual Difference in *The Handmaid's Tale*' in *Litterature* Vol. 6, parts 3–4 (December, 1995), pp. 233–256.

Sarah R. Morrison, 'Mothering Desire: The Romance Plot in Margaret Atwood's *The Handmaid's Tale* and Susan Fromberg Schaeffer's *The Madness of a Seduced Woman*', *Tulsa Studies in Women's Literature*, vol. 19, part 2, (Fall, 2000) pp. 315–336

Bob Myhal, 'Boundaries, Centers and Circles: The Postmodern Geometry of *The Handmaid's Tale*' in *Litterature* (December, 1995), pp. 213–231.

Colin Nicholson (ed.), *Margaret Atwood: Writing and Subjectivity* (Macmillan, Basingstoke, 1994).

Reingard M. Nischik, 'Nomenclatural Mutations: Forms of Address in Margaret Atwood's Novels', in *Orbis Litterarum: International Review of Literary Studies* Vol 52, part 5 (1997), pp. 329–351.

Emma Parker, '"You Are What You Eat": The Politics of Eating in the Novels of Margaret Atwood', in *Twentieth Century Literature*, Vol. 42 part 3, (Fall, 1995), pp. 349–368.

Vernon Provencal, '"Byzantine in the Extreme"' Plato's *Republic* in *The Handmaid's Tale*' in *Classical and Modern Literature: A Quarterly*, Vol. 19, part 1 (Fall, 1998), pp. 53–76.

Jeanne Campbell Reesman, 'Dark Knowledge in *The Handmaid's Tale*', in *Critic* Vol. 53 (3), (Spring–Summer, 1991), pp. 6–22.

Helene A Shugart, 'Counterhegemonic Acts: Appropriation as Feminist Rhetorical Strategy', *Quarterly Journal of Speech*, Vol. 83, part 2, (May, 1997), pp. 210–229.

Hilde Staels, 'Margaret Atwood's *The Handmaid's Tale:* Resistance Through Narrating'. in *English Studies* Vol. 78, part 6 (September 1995), pp. 455–467.

Hilde Staels, 'The Eclipse of "The Other Voice": Margaret Atwood's *The Handmaid's Tale*', in *Litteratures et Civilisations du Monde Anglophone*, Vol. 8, (October, 1988), pp. 203–206.

Karen Stein, 'Margaret Atwood's Modest Proposal', in *Canadian Literature*, vol. 148, (Spring, 1996), pp. 57–73.

N. Stein, *Margaret Atwood* (Twayne Modern Author Series, New York, 2001)

Charlotte Sturgess, 'Manipulating Cliches: Margaret Atwood's Romance Narrative Bluebeard's Egg', in *GRAAT: Publication des Groupes de Recherches Anglo Americaines de L'Universite Francois Rabelais de Tours*, Vol. 16 (1997), pp. 143–148.

Rosemary Sullivan, *The Red Shoes: Margaret Atwood Starting Out* (Harper Flamingo, Toronto, 1998).

Sheldon Teitelbaum, 'The Handmaid's Tale: The Film' Cinefantastique, Vol. 20, part 4 (March 1990).

Charlotte Templin, 'Names and Naming Tell an Archetypal Story in Margaret Atwood's The Handmaid's Tale' in Canadian Literature Vol. 138–139, (Fall–Winter, 1993), pp. 147–157.

Sandra Tomc, '"The Missionary Position": Feminism and Nationalism in Margaret Atwood's The Handmaid's Tale', in Names: A Journal of Onomastics Vol. 41 (3), (September 1993), pp. 147–157.

Toni Wein, 'Margaret Atwood's Historical Notes', in Notes on Contemporary Literature, Vol. 25, part 2 (March 1995), pp. 2–3.

Also available in Vintage

Margaret Atwood

DANCING GIRLS

'A remarkable collection'
Sunday Times

Pregnant women, students and journalists; farmers, bird-watchers, ex-wives, adolescent lovers – and dancing girls. All ordinary people – or are they?

Margaret Atwood's distinctive wit and incisive observation of the strangeness of everyday life makes this a delightfully absorbing collection of stories. She portrays each drama with tremendous agility that seems effortless, and makes it impossible to stop at the end of one story without dipping into the next.

'Margaret Atwood's stories are fierce parables about the horror of city life and the power politics of relationships. The fierceness filters insidiously through the leisurely realism of her domestic interiors, clothes, meals, weather . . . A remarkable collection' Victoria Glendinning,
Sunday Times

'An acute and poetic observer of the eternal, universal, rum relationships between men and women'
The Times

'The mind revealed in this collection of short stories is acutely perceptive, in love with language and capable of seeing significant connections between apparently disparate circumstances'
Sheila Macleod, *Evening Standard*

'If anyone has a better insight into women and their central problem – men – than Margaret Atwood, and can voice them with as much wit, impact and grace, then they haven't started writing yet'
Daily Mail

Also available in Vintage

Margaret Atwood

LIFE BEFORE MAN

'A splendid work'
Marilyn French

Elizabeth, monstrous yet pitiable; Nate, her husband, a patch-work man, gentle, disillusioned; Lesje, a young woman at the natural history museum, for whom dinosaurs are as important as men. A sexual triangle; three people in thrall to the tragi-comedy we call love . . .

Few writers are as skilled as Margaret Atwood at reading into the minds and lives of their characters – disclosing, with such faultless artistry, disturbingly familiar truths about ourselves.

'A modern saga . . . she has a fine ear for words and a quick wit for absurdities"
The Times

'An extraordinary imagination – witty, light-footed, realistic, yet with shooting insights into the nature of personality and love'
Financial Times

'Tender, funny, absorbing, idiosyncratic, truthful, heartening – it is a liberating novel. It deserves a wide readership'
Literary Review

'Mordant intelligence; formidable insight into the springs of human self-deception, self-aggrandisement and self-destruction; and an effortless, always vivid style'
Spectator

'Beautifully written and constructed . . . a rich and elegant achievement'.
Peter Kemp, *Listener*

Also available in Vintage

Margaret Atwood

BODILY HARM

'One of the most richly entertaining novels I've read for years'
Guardian

'As swift-moving as the best thriller, clipped and laconic, yet deeply and richly sensitive'
Sunday Telegraph

'A beautifully written, witty and often poignant account of a brave woman's attempt to come to terms with her situation and recover her spirits'
Nina Bawden, *Daily Telegraph*

'What makes her book so considerable an achievement is the mature, informed accuracy of its view of life. What makes it so exhilarating is the profusion of tough wit and precise poetry that everywhere transforms its black bulletins from documentary into art'
Peter Kemp, *Times Literary Supplement*

'The only way to describe my response to *Bodily Harm* is to say that it knocked me out . . . She tosses off perfect scenes with a casualness that leaves you utterly unprepared for the way these stories seize you'
New York Times

BY MARGARET ATWOOD
ALSO AVAILABLE IN VINTAGE

☐ *Dancing Girls*	Margaret Atwood	£6.99
☐ *Life Before Man*	Margaret Atwood	£6.99
☐ *Bodily Harm*	Margaret Atwood	£6.99
☐ *Bluebeard's Egg*	Margaret Atwood	£6.99
☐ *The Handmaid's Tale*	Margaret Atwood	£6.99

- All Vintage books are available through mail order or from your local bookshop.
- Payment may be made using Access, Visa, Mastercard, Diners Club, Switch and Amex, or cheque, eurocheque and postal order (sterling only).

☐☐☐☐☐☐☐☐☐☐☐☐☐☐☐

Expiry Date:_____ Signature:_____

Please allow £2.50 for post and packing for the first book and £1.00 per book thereafter.

ALL ORDERS TO:
Vintage Books, Books by Post, TBS Limited, The Book Service,
Colchester Road, Frating Green, Colchester, Essex, CO7 7DW, UK.
Telephone: (01206) 256 000
Fax:　　　 (01206) 255 914

NAME: _____

ADDRESS: _____

_____

_____

Please allow 28 days for delivery. Please tick box if you do not wish to
receive any additional information.　　　　　　　　　　　　　　　　☐
Prices and availability subject to change without notice.